uNEASY NEIGHBORS

UNEASY NEIGHBORS

CUBA AND THE UNITED STATES

RHODA HOFF AND MARGARET REGLER

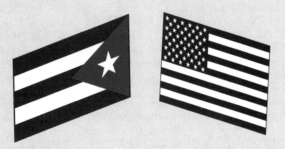

FRANKLIN WATTS
New York ▪ Chicago ▪ London ▪ Toronto ▪ Sydney
Danbury, Connecticut

Interior Design: Molly Heron

Photographs ©: AP/Wide World Photos: 93, 166, 172; Archive Photos: 69, 115, 117, 119, 135, 138, 153; Corbis-Bettmann: 20, 27; Miami Herald Publishing Co.: 156; North Wind Picture Archives: 39; Reuters/Archive Photos: 174; Reuters/Corbis-Bettmann: 169; Stock Montage, Inc.: 66; UPI/Corbis-Bettmann: 88, 106, 129, 149.

For information on the permissions for the use of works excerpted in this book, please refer to the acknowledgments page.

Library of Congress Cataloging-in-Publication Data
    Hoff, Rhoda.
    Uneasy Neighbors: Cuba and the United States / by Rhoda Hoff and Margaret Regler.
        p. cm
    Includes bibliographical references and index.
    ISBN 0-531-11326-4
    1. Cuba–History–1895–Sources–Juvenile literature. 2. Self-determination.   National–Cuba–History–Sources–Juvenile   literature.   3. Cuba–Relations–United States–Sources–Juvenile literature. 4. United States–
    Relations–Cuba–Sources– Juvenile   literature. [1. Cuba–History–Sources. 2. Cuba–Relations–United States–Sources. 3. United States–Relations–Cuba–Sources.] I. Regler, Margaret. II. Title.

F1787.H64   1997   92-41174
327.7291073–dc20   CIP
                                                            AC

ACKNOWLEDGMENTS

We would like to thank the New York Society Library and its librarians for their informed help and patience in assembling the material for this book. We would also like to thank the New York Public Library for permission to use the Wertheim room which made our research both more efficient and more enjoyable.

The following publishers have kindly given permission to use excerpts from the following works: From *The Cuban Story*, by Herbert Matthews, copyright © 1961. Reprinted by permission of George Braziller. From *The Great Deception*, by James Monahan and Kenneth Gilmore, copyright © 1963. Reprinted by permission of Farrar, Straus & Giroux. From *The Fish is Red*, by Warren Hinckle and William Turner, copyright © 1981. Reprinted by permission of Harper-Collins. From *Against All Hope*, by Armando Valladeres, copyright © 1986. Reprinted by permission of Alfred A. Knopf. From *Guerrilla Prince*, by Georgie Ann Geyer, copyright © 1991. Reprinted by permission of Little Brown. From *Fidel: A Critical Portrait*, by Tad Szulc, copyright ©1986. Reprinted by permission of William Morrow. From *Miami*, by Joan Didion, copyright © 1987. Reprinted by permission of Simon & Schuster.

CONTENTS

INTRODUCTION

On October 28, 1492, Christopher Columbus, exploring for Spain, anchored his ships off the island of Cuba. He wrote in his diary that "the prospect here exceeded in beauty anything I have ever seen." Almost three hundred and thirty-one years later to the day, Thomas Jefferson, from his retirement in Monticello in Virginia, wrote President James Monroe that he favored the president's contemplated doctrine whose object was to "keep out all foreign powers." But, Jefferson confessed, "my greatest regret" is that in sponsoring the Monroe Doctrine, the United States must surrender all claim to Cuba which, Jefferson wrote, "I have ever looked upon as the most interesting addition which could ever be made to our system of states."

Throughout the tangled history of U.S.–Cuban relations, it was more than the beauty of the island that attracted us to Cuba. Cuba's strategic location was the overruling consideration. The distance from Key West, off the Florida coast, to the northwest coast of Cuba is only eighty-six miles, the same distance that separates Washington from Philadelphia. In addition, Cuba controls not only the entire Caribbean but also the entrance to the Gulf of Mexico and the Panama Canal. Small wonder that for four hundred years Cuba has been a prize desired not only by the United States but by foreign powers as well.

Uneasy Neighbors will not attempt to present a complete history of the interwoven fortunes of Cuba and the United States, complicated as they have been at various times and still are today by war, clashing economic interests, conflicting ideologies, and crises of various kinds. From Columbus to Castro, the United States has never ceased for long to be involved in Cuba's affairs.

The materials gathered together in this book have been selected, like points on a graph, to plot the curve of Cuban-U.S. relations from a day in 1492 when Christopher Columbus anchored off that beautiful island to a time almost five hundred years later when Cuba and the United States have become estranged by conflicting ideologies and are searching for the way to a happier future.

Many of the articles included in this book were written by men and women who were reporting something they themselves had seen, heard, or experienced. Richard Harding Davis, a famous war correspondent of his day, described Theodore Roosevelt and his Rough Riders as they stormed San Juan Hill; a latter-day *New York Times* correspondent, Herbert Matthews, told of his secret meeting with a young Fidel Castro, who at the time was still hiding in the mountains and had not yet come to power. These are examples of history with a small h. It is an exciting and flavorful approach, but it must, by its very nature, be something of an adventure. It is a contact with the past that is amazingly alive.

In addition to the personal accounts that constitute the bulk of the book, there is a selection of official reports, acts of Congress, treaties, and other documents to fortify the small *h* of the eyewitness with the capital *H* of the historian. Together, eyewitness and historian will tell the unfinished story of two uneasy neighbors as they continue their long search for a *modus vivendi.*

THE DIARY OF
CHRISTOPHER COLUMBUS[1]

In 1492, Columbus undertook the epic voyage that changed the world. On October 12, Columbus anchored his ships near a small island, now known as Cuba. The excerpt Cuba that follows is taken from his diary, written at the time of his discovery. Columbus was enchanted by the natural beauty of his surroundings, and until his death, he was convinced that he had reached China. From his first voyage to Cuba in 1492, he wrote, "A thousand tongues would not suffice to describe the things of novelty and beauty I saw, for it was all like a scene of enchantment."

Sunday, October 28, 1492: Continued on SSW. In quest of the island of CUBA, keeping close to the shore. Entered a fine river, free from shallows and all other obstructions, which in fact is the case with all the coast here, the shore being very bold. The mouth of the river had a depth of water of twelve fathoms, and a breadth sufficient for ships to beat in. They anchored within the river, and the admiral states that the prospect here exceeded in beauty anything he ever saw, the river being surrounded with trees of the most beautiful and luxuriant foliage of a singular appearance, and covered with flowers and fruits of all sorts. Birds were here in abundance singing most delightfully. Great numbers of pine trees were noticed, different from those of Guinea, and ours, wanting their particular manner of bark; they were of a moderate height, and bore very large leaves, which the natives use for coverings to their homes. The land appeared quite level. The admiral went ashore in the boat, and found two dwellings, which he supposed to be those of fisherman, and that the owners had fled. He found in one of them a dog unable to bark. Both houses contained nets of palm, lines, horn fishhooks, harpoons of bone, and other implements for fishing, also many fireplaces, and each seemed to be adapted to the reception of a large number of persons. The admiral gave orders that nothing should be touched, which directions were adhered to. The grass was as high as it is in Andalusia in May, and they found purslain and strawberry-blight in abundance. They returned on board the boat and ascended the river some distance, where the admiral says it was exceedingly pleasant to behold the delightful foliage and verdure which presented itself, not to mention the birds in the neighborhood; the whole offered a scene of such enchantment that it was hardly possible to part from it. He declared this to be the most beautiful island ever seen, abounding in good harbors, and deep rivers, with a shore upon which it appears that the sea never breaks high, as the grass grows down to the water's edge, a thing which never happens where the sea is rough. Indeed a high sea they had not as yet experienced among these islands. This isle, he says, is full of pleasant mountains, which are lofty, although not of great extent, the rest of the country is high, after the manner of Sicily, abounding in streams, as they understood from the Indians of Guanahani, which were on board the ships . . . that it contained ten large rivers, and was of such a size that with their canoes they could not sail around it in twenty days. When the ships were sailing towards the island, some of the natives put off from the shore in two canoes, and perceiving the Spaniards entering into the boat and rowing towards the mouth of the river to sound for an anchorage, they took to flight. The Indians told them there were mines of gold here and pearls, and the admiral observed mussels and other indications of these articles in the neighborhood. They further informed him that there came large ships hither from the Great Can, and the mainland was distant ten days' voyage. The admiral named this river and port San Salvador.

A LETTER FROM JOHN QUINCY ADAMS TO THE AMERICAN MINISTER TO SPAIN[2]

The island of Cuba, lying only about ninety miles south of Florida, is strategically situated to dominate the only two entrances to the Gulf of Mexico. From the outset, Cuba has been a source of concern to the government and people of the United States.

As one writer put it, "If England had held it during the American Revolution, it would doubtless have delayed the success of the American Colonies. It was there that many of the fleets which harmed England found a harbor."

In 1823, John Quincy Adams, secretary of state under President James Monroe and one of the authors of the Monroe Doctrine, which played such an important part in the history of the United States, wrote the following letter in which he stressed that Cuba had an "importance in the sum of our national interests with which no other foreign territory can be compared."

April 28, 1823: Cuba, almost in sight of our shores, from a multitude of considerations, has become an object of transcendent importance to the commercial and political interests of our Union. Its commanding positions, with reference to the Gulf of Mexico and the West Indies seas; the character of its population; its situation midway between our southern coast and the island of St. Domingo; its safe and spacious harbor of Havana, fronting a long line of our shores destitute of the same advantage; the nature of its productions and of its wants, furnishing the supplies and needing the returns of a commerce immensely profitable and mutually beneficial, gives it an importance in the sum of our national interests with which that of no other foreign territory can be compared, and little inferior to that which binds the different members of this Union together. Such, indeed, are, between the interests of that island and of this country, the geographical, commercial, moral, and political relations, formed by nature, gathering in the process of time, and even now verging to maturity, that, in looking forward to the probable course of events, for the short period of half a century, it is scarcely possible to resist the conviction that the annexation of Cuba to our federal republic will be indispensable to the continuance and integrity of the Union itself. It is obvious, however, that for this event we are not yet prepared. Numerous and formidable objections to the extension of our territorial dominions beyond the sea present themselves to the first contemplation of the subject; obstacles to the system of policy by which alone that result can be compassed and maintained, are to be foreseen and surmounted, both from at home and abroad, but there are laws of political, as well as physical gravitation; and if an apple, severed by the tempest from its native tree, cannot choose but to fall to the ground, Cuba, forcibly disjoined from its own unnatural connection with Spain, and incapable of self-support, can gravitate only towards the North American Union, which, by the same law of nature, cannot cast her off from its bosom.

U.S. House, Exec. Doc. 32nd Cong., 1st Sess.

THE VIRGINIUS AFFAIR

From 1868 to 1878, Cuban patriots fought stubbornly to win their independence from a tyrannical Spanish government. The American people sided with the island patriots, but the U.S. government decided to remain neutral. José Martí, Tomás Estrada Palma, and many other Cuban sympathizers living in the United States not only raised money for the patriot cause but also attempted to send supplies of all kinds to the revolutionaries in chartered American ships that sailed from American ports. Some of the ships managed to elude the authorities, but the majority were intercepted by U.S. authorities and prevented from sailing.

In 1869 the Spanish government ordered the capture of any ship caught carrying supplies to the revolutionaries and demanded the execution as pirates of any passengers on the boats. America refused to allow such actions unless war had been officially declared.

The situation threatened to explode in 1873 when the *Virginius,* a former U.S. ship that had been bought by Cuban sympathizers and loaded with war supplies, was captured on the high seas. The *Virginius* was flying the American flag at the time. Taken to Santiago by the Spanish authorities, the captain of the *Virginius* and fifty-one others, some of them Americans, were summarily shot to death.

The American press reported this barbarous event in gory detail. Led by the sensational "yellow press," the American people demanded that the United States go to war with Spain.

The U.S. government issued an ultimatum, demanding that General Burriel, the Spanish commander, be punished; the families of the murdered crew be suitably indemnified; and that there be a salute to the American flag.

A year later, there was a compromise. The Spanish

government paid an indemnity of eighty thousand dollars to the families of the executed men. America waived the salute to the flag. General Burriel was never punished as Spain had promised, however, and eventually he was even promoted.

The New York Herald Reports on the Capture of the American Steamship Virginius[3]

November 5, 1873: The American steamship *Virginius* was captured with all on board, by the Spanish gunboat *Tornado* on the 31st of October 1873.

She had 170 passengers and crew who with the vessel and cargo have been brought to Santiago, Cuba.

Proceeding commenced against the prisoners.

Particulars from Santiago: The *Tornado* had been searching for the *Virginius* since her attempt to land on the island. The *Virginius* then put on full steam and made for Jamaica, hoping for refuge in British waters. In her flight, she threw overboard horses and a portion of fuel. The *Tornado* caught up with her near the Jamaican coast. She was surrounded with all on board; no one escaped. Among those captured was the well-known Captain Bambetts, who was reported killed a few days ago.

The prisoners have all been brought before a competent tribunal at Santiago and are being tried as pirates.

There is rejoicing in Havana over the news. Streets and houses decorated.

November 8: The Santiago Tribunal shoots four prisoners.

November 9: The Spanish commanding general, Burriel, reports the execution of the prisoners shot to death in the presence of an immense concourse of citizens, soldiers, and sailors. The prisoners met their death with composure.

November 12: Washington says it's time to inter-fere. President Grant is in favor of mediation between Spain and Cuba.

November 13: Captain and crew executed by Spaniards. Forty-nine persons shot to death. Bloody scene at Santiago.

November 14: Our entire force of warships getting ready for sea. Congress expected to act.

November 15: Spanish barbarism: 57 more shot, 18 out of 163 to be spared. The government in Washing-ton in session organizing the naval forces.

November 16: Santiago butchers murder Captain Fry. General American indignation. Captain Fry was a noble-looking old man. The Spanish marines took seven minutes to kill 37 of the wretched prisoners. It seemed as if they would never finish. The death carts were hurried up and loaded indiscriminately with the mangled remains.

November 19: Fifteen of the *Virginius* passengers sentenced to prison.

November 27: Ultimatum: America demands full reparations.

The Virginius Affair by Gonzalo de Quesada[4]
Gonzalo de Quesada was the Cuban
chargé d'affaires in Washington, D.C.

In October 1873 the *Virginius* was captured by the Spanish in neutral waters, near the British Island of Jamaica. It was towed

The crew of the Virginius *await execution. The ship was seized by the Spanish in 1873 because it brought war supplies to Cuba to help that country's efforts to win independence from a tyrannical Spanish government. After its capture, the captain and 51 others were shot to death.*

into Santiago de Cuba, declared a pirate ship, and fifty-two of the officers and crew were executed against the protest of the United States consul. The whole thing was irregular. A fraudulent use was made of the Stars and Stripes.

The incident served to inform the world of the wholesale lawless butchery going on in Cuba. The four principal officers were marched to the slaughter house of Santiago de Cuba and murdered. They were made to kneel, facing the wall. As they fell into the ditch the cavalry rode over their warm bodies, and military wagons crunched and slipped on the bodies. Negroes cut off their heads and carried them on pikes through the city, and the mutilated bodies were dumped into a pit of quicklime.

The North American continent thrilled with indignation. In view of the outrage, war between Spain and the United States seemed to be imminent and unavoidable.

It was soon apparent that the government in Washington did not mean business any further than requiring the surrender of the *Virginius* and the surviving members of her crew, and an indemnity trivial in amount, for the blood of those American citizens whose nationality could be proved beyond peradventure.

From the versatile pen of Major Moses P. Hardy we quote the following graphic description of the bloody tragedy:

We left Key West on a Sunday night at ten o'clock. I managed to get at the secret, and, thus armed, stowed away on the *Dispatch,* which was the vessel appointed to receive the surrender. We were in the open sea before I ventured to make my appearance on deck, present myself to the officers, declare myself a stowaway, and verify my information as to their mission. The next morning at ten o'clock the blue of the Cuban coast rose above the horizon, and the bow of the boat was directed toward Hahia Honda, the obscure little port selected for the function. It was about noon when we passed an old fort commanding the entrance to the harbor, speed was then slackened, and the vessel crept cautiously along a narrow but clearly marked channel, which leads to the smooth water where the *Virginius* was supposed to be lying. As soon as our boat was sighted from the shore, the Spanish flag was flung to the breeze. We discovered a black side-wheel steamship lying about a mile beyond the fort. It was the *Virginius,* and immediately the Stars and Stripes were raised by Spanish hands and again floated over the vessel, which also carried the unfortunate comrades to their death.

After an exchange of courteous salutations, the Spanish captain remarked that he had received a copy of the protocol providing for the surrender of the *Virginius* and that the surrender might now be considered to have taken place. Our captain replied that under his instructions the following day was named for the surrender, and that he could not receive it until then. Meanwhile he would thank the Spanish officer to continue in possession. Nine o'clock on Tuesday morning was then agreed upon as the hour, and after informing the American officer that there was coal enough on board of the *Virginius* to last six days, salutes were exchanged and the Spanish officer retired.

The next morning, half an hour ahead of time, a gig came over to the *Virginius.* It contained a single officer and an oarsman. As the officer stepped on deck, a petty officer and half a dozen men, who had stood watch on the *Virginius* during the night, went over the side and remained in a dinghy awaiting orders. At 9:00 precisely by the bells, the American flag again flew to the flagstaff of the *Virginius,* and at the same moment two officers put away from the *Dispatch.* As they ascended the accommodation ladder of the *Virginius,* the single man on deck advanced and made a courteous salute.

The officers then read their respective instructions, and the Spanish captain remarked that in obedience to the requirements of the government and in execution of the provisions of the protocol, he had the honor to turn over the steamer *Virginius* to the American authorities.

While the Spanish officer was courtesy itself, we were all impressed with the fact that the ceremony was lacking in dignity and that the Spaniards had purposely made the lack as conspicuous as they dared.

A quick survey by our officers showed the *Virginius* to be in a most filthy condition. She was stripped of almost everything movable, save a few vermin, which haunted the mattresses and the cushions in the cabin and staterooms and half a dozen casks of water. The decks were caked with dirt, and nuisances recently committed combined with mold and decomposition to cause a foul stench in the forecastle and below the hatches. Our officers were reluctant to put the men into the dirty forecastle by the staterooms of their butchered companions. After a few hours of hard work we got under way, but had only gone 200 yards when the engines suddenly refused to do duty and it became necessary for the *Dispatch* to take us in tow. We had a hard time that night, those of us who were aboard the *Virginius*. It seemed hardly possible that we could keep afloat until morning.

During the night a navy tug, *Fortune*, from Key West, met us and remained with the convoy. At noon the next day, when we were about 30 miles south of Dry Tortugas, the vessels separated, the *Virginius* and the *Dispatch* going to Tortugas and the *Fortune* returning with me as a solitary passenger to Key West whence I had the honor of reporting the news to the admiral. An attempt was made to take the *Virginius* to some northern port, but the old hulk was not equal to the journey, and on the way no pumping or caulking could stop her leaks, and she foundered in mid-ocean.

The surrender of the surviving prisoners took place in the course of time in Santiago—never to this day has there been any adequate atonement by Spain, much less an apology or expression of regret for the *Virginius* massacre.

MY RACE BY JOSE MARTI[5]

One of the true heroes of Cuba's long struggle for freedom was the poet-patriot José Martí. A boy of fifteen during the first year of the Ten Year War, he was arrested in Havana for writing seditious poetry. He was sentenced to six years at hard labor in the quarries, "to work shackled with chain and ball." In 1871, influence was exerted on his behalf and his sentence was commuted to "permanent exile." Deported to Spain, he was permitted to study at the University of Madrid where he devoted most of his time and energy to making speeches on behalf of Cuba's freedom and writing articles to further his cause.

His sentence was later commuted again. Forbidden to return to Cuba but allowed to travel, he lived for some years in South America, then came to the United States where he made New York City his headquarters. From this base, he traveled extensively, collecting money and ammunition to promote the cause of Cuban freedom. Fiery, magnetic, and eloquent, Martí persuaded even the tough Cuban cigar makers in Florida to sacrifice for the common cause. Women, too, gave their gold wedding rings to help raise money. In New York, together with his friend Tomás Estrada Palma, who later became the first president of Cuba, Martí roused the weak Cuban junta to new and active life.

José Martí did not believe in racial discrimination. Again and again he rose to the defense of the black man. "Do not accuse him of inferiority as a slave race," he told his fellow Cubans, "because the white, blue-eyed, blond-haired Gauls were sold as serfs with collars around their necks in the marketplace of Rome."

The credo on race that follows was first printed in *Patria*, the newspaper Martí helped to found. *Patria* was the official organ of the Cuban Revolutionary party in the United States. Until 1895 Martí himself edited the paper.

The word "racist" has taken on a confused meaning, and it must be clarified. A man has no particular rights because he happens to belong to one particular race; when one says "man," that should include all rights. A Negro is neither inferior nor superior to another because he is black; the white man carries redundancy too far when he says "my race," and so does the Negro when he makes the same statements. Everything that divides men, everything that herds men together in categories, is a sin against humanity. What sensible white man would think of taking pride in being white, and what must the Negro think of the white man who is proud of being white and feels he has special privileges as a result? What must the white man think of the Negro who takes pride in his color? Always to dwell on the divisions or differences between the races, in people who are sufficiently divided already, is to raise barriers to the attainment of both national and individual well-being, for those two goals are reached by bringing together as closely as possible the various components that form the nation. . . .

In Cuba there is no fear whatever of racial conflict. A man is more than white, black, or mulatto. A Cuban is more than mulatto, black, or white. Dying for Cuba on the battlefield, the souls of both Negroes and white men have risen together. In the daily life of defense, loyalty, brotherhood, and shrewdness, there has always been a Negro standing beside every white man. Negroes as well as white men classify themselves according to their characteristics: bravery or timidity, selfishness or unselfishness. . . .

And as for the rest, each one will be free in the sanctity of his own household. Merit, the manifest and continuous evidence of culture, and the constant process of trade will eventually unite all men. There is a plentiful supply of greatness in Cuba, in Negroes and white men alike.

A VINDICATION OF CUBA
BY JOSE MARTI[6]

On March 16, 1889 under the title "Do We Want Cuba?", an article had appeared in the *Manufacturer,* a Philadelphia newspaper. The article was insulting to Cuba and Cubans and ended with the statement: "Our only hope of qualifying Cuba for the dignity of statehood would be to Americanize her completely."

José Martí, the patriot and poet, was at that time living in exile in New York City and lecturing throughout the United States. Indignant at the aspersions cast against Cuba and Cubans in the *Manufacturer* article, he rose to the defense of his countrymen.

His article, "A Vindication of Cuba," was a refutation of the accusations made in the *Manufacturer* article, which had been reproduced in the *New York Evening Post.* Martí's article was printed in the *Post* on March 25, 1889. It was written in English.

The following is an excerpt from Martí's article.

José Martí, poet and patriot, was the greatest hero
in Cuba's long struggle for freedom.

To the Editor of the *New York Evening Post:*

The Cubans have, according to the *Manufacturer* article of March 16, 1889, "a distaste for exertion": they are "helpless," "idle." These "helpless," "idle" men came here twenty years ago empty-handed, with very few exceptions, fought against the climate, mastered the language, lived by their honest labor, some in affluence, a few in wealth, rarely in misery, they bought and built homes, they raised families and fortunes, they loved luxury, and worked for it; they were not frequently seen in the dark roads of life; proud and self-sustaining, they never feared competition as to intelligence or diligence. Thousands have returned to die in their homes, thousands have remained where, during the hardships of life, they have triumphed, unaided by any help of kindred language, sympathy of race, or community of religion. A handful of Cuban toilers built Key West. The Cubans have made their mark in Panama by their ability as mechanics of the higher trades, as clerks, physicians, and contractors. A Cuban, Cisneros, has greatly advanced the development of railroads and river navigation in Colombia. Marquez, another Cuban, gained with many of his countrymen the respect of the Peruvians as a merchant of eminent capacity. Cubans are found everywhere, working as farmers, surveyors, engineers, mechanics, teachers, journalists. In Philadelphia, the *Manufacturer* has a daily opportunity to see a hundred Cubans, some of them of heroic history and powerful build, who live by their work in easy comfort.

In New York the Cubans are directors in prominent banks, substantial merchants, popular brokers, clerks of recognized ability, physicians with a large practice, engineers of worldwide repute, electricians, journalists, tradesmen, cigar makers. The poet of Niagara is a Cuban. R. Heredia . . . is a projector of the canal of Nicaragua. In Philadelphia itself, as in New York, the college prizes have more than once been awarded to Cubans. The women of these "helpless, idle" people with "a distaste for exertion" arrived here from a life of luxury in the heart of the winter; their husbands were in the war, ruined, dead, imprisoned in Spain. The senora went to work. From a slave owner she became a slave, took a seat behind the counter, sang in the churches, worked buttonholes by the hundred, sewed for a living, curled feathers, gave her soul to duty, withered in work her body. This is the people of defective morals. . . .

It is finally said [in the Philadelphia article] that our lack of manly force and self-respect is demonstrated by the suppleness with which we have so long submitted to Spanish oppression, and even our intensive rebellions have been so pitifully ineffective that they have risen little above the dignity of farce. Never was ignorance of history and character more pitifully displayed than in this wanton assertion. We need to recollect, in order to answer without bitterness, that more than one American bled by our side, in a war that another American was to call a farce. A farce! The war that has been by foreign observers, compared to an epic, the upheaval of a whole country, the voluntary abandonment of wealth, the abolition of slavery in our first moment of freedom, the burning of our cities by our own hands, the erection of villages and factories in the wild forest, the keeping at bay, in ten years of such a life, a powerful enemy, with a loss to him in figures of 200,000 men, at the hands of a small army of patriots, with no help but nature! We had no Hessians and no Frenchmen, no Lafayette or Stueben, no monarchial rivals to help us. We had but one neighbor who confessedly "stretched the limits of its power and acted against the will of the people" to help the foes of those who were fighting for the same Chartered Liberties on which he built his independence. We fell a victim to the very passions which could have caused the downfall of the thirteen States, had they not been cemented by success, while we were enfeebled by procrastination, a procrastination brought about, not from cowardice, but from a torrent of blood, which allowed the enemy in the first months of the war to acquire unconquerable advantage, and from a childlike confidence in the certain help of the United States. They cannot see us dying for liberty at their own doors without raising a hand or saying a word to give to the world a new free country! They did not raise the hand. They did not say the word.

The struggle has not ceased. The exiles do not want to return. The new generation is worthy of its sires.

WINSTON CHURCHILL JOINS THE ARMY BY WINSTON CHURCHILL[7]

"In the closing decade of the Victorian era, the Empire had enjoyed so long a spell of almost unbroken peace that medals and all they represented in experience and adventure, were becoming scarce in the British army." So wrote Winston Churchill, then a young officer in Her Majesty's Tenth Hussars. War service was the swiftest road to promotion, but at that time there was no war being waged in Europe. So, cognizant of the fact that two and a half months of winter leave was coming due and that he had spent all his money on polo ponies, young Churchill, as he put it, "searched the world for some scene of adventure and excitement."

In Cuba, he discovered, the Spanish army was still fighting the rebels. "From early youth," Churchill writes, "I had imagined the sensation attendant upon being for the first time under fire. It must be a thrilling and immense experience to hear the whistle of bullets all around and to play at hazard from moment to moment with death and wounds."

Ever the man of action, the young Churchill and a brother officer soon activated their plan. With the help of the British ambassador to Spain, a friend of Churchill's late father, they obtained excellent introductions, both formal and personal, together with the ambassador's assurance that the two young officers had only to reach Havana to receive a warm welcome from the Spanish general in command. So, at the beginning of November 1895, Churchill and his friend sailed for New York and from there to Havana.

"Cuba is a lovely island," Churchill wrote on arriving in Havana, "well have the Spaniards named it 'the Pearl of the Antilles.' The temperate yet ardent climate, the abundant rainfall, the luxurious vegetation, the unrivaled fertility of the soil, the beautiful scenery—all combined to make me accuse the absentminded morning when our ancestors let so delectable a possession slip through our fingers. However, our modern democracy has inherited enough—to keep or to cast away."

The letters of introduction were handed over and, as the ambassador had predicted, were enthusiastically received. The very next morning the two young British officers were on their way to join the forces of General Valdez. The journey would take three days, but as Churchill wrote, it was "accomplished with some risk but no accident."

General Valdez, Churchill wrote, "welcomed the two young officers most cordially. He explained, through an interpreter, what an honor it was for him to have two distinguished representatives of a great and friendly power attached to his column, and how highly he valued the moral support which this great gesture by Great Britain implied."

Soon Churchill was to have what he had longed for: his first experience of being under fire.

We slept on the night of November 29 in the fortified village of Arroyo Blanco. We had sent two battalions and one squadron with the main part of the convoy to carry provisions to a series of garrisons. The rest of our force, numbering perhaps 1,700 men, were to seek the enemy and fight. The thirtieth of November was my twenty-first birthday, and on that day for the first time I heard shots fired in anger and heard bullets strike flesh or whistle through the air.

There was excitement and commotion. A party of soldiers rushed to the place whence the volley had been fired and of course found nothing except a few empty cartridge cases. Meanwhile I had been meditating upon the wounded horse. It was a chestnut. The bullet had struck between the ribs, the blood dripped on the ground, and there was a circle of dark red on his chestnut coat about a foot wide. He hung his head but did not fall. Evidently, however, he was going to die, for his saddle and bridle were soon taken off him. As I watched these proceedings, I could not help reflecting that the bullet which had struck the chestnut had certainly passed within a foot of my head. So, at any rate, I had been "under fire." That was something. Nevertheless, I began to take a more thoughtful view of our enterprise than I had hitherto done.

After about half an hour, the insurgents had had enough and went off, carrying away with them the wounded and the dead.

We dined undisturbed on the veranda and returned to our hammocks in a little barn. I was soon awakened by firing. A bullet ripped through the thatch of our hut, another wounded an orderly just outside. I should have been glad to get out of my hammock and lie on the ground. However, as no one else moved, I thought it more becoming to stay where I was. I fortified myself by dwelling on the fact that the Spanish officer whose hammock was slung between me and the enemy fire, was a man of substantial physique; indeed one might have almost called him fat. I have never been prejudiced against fat men. At any rate, I did not begrudge this one his meals. Gradually I dropped asleep.

After a disturbed night, the column started early in the morning. The enemy, falling back before us, took advantage of every position. . . . The firing on both sides became heavy. There were sounds about us sometimes like a sigh, sometimes like a whistle, and at others like the buzz of an offended hornet. The general and his staff rode forward until the smoke-crackling fence was only four or five hundred yards away. Here we halted, and sitting mounted, without the slightest cover or concealment, watched the assault of the infantry. During this period, the air was full of whizzings, and the palm trees smitten by the bullets yielded resounding smacks and thuds. The Spaniards were on their mettle, and we had to do our best to keep up appearances. It really seemed very dangerous indeed, and I was astonished to see how few people were hit amid all this clatter. In our group of about twenty, only three or four horses and men were wounded, and not one killed.

As our column had now only one day's rations left, we withdrew across the plain. Spanish honor and our own curiosity alike being satisfied, the column returned to the coast to La Jicotea, and we to England. We did not think the Spaniards were likely to bring their war in Cuba to a speedy end.

MARTI'S LAST DAY
BY JOSE MARTI[8]

In the spring of 1895, José Martí, the Cuban poet-patriot, decided that the time had come to free Cuba. His fellow revolutionaries felt that, as he had never been a soldier, he could best serve the cause by remaining in the United States to raise popular support. But Martí himself felt that only a taste of gunfire would prevent his enemies from calling him a "rice powder patriot." A compromise was reached: Martí would take part in the invasion but would remain in Cuba only a short time.

From New York he first traveled to the cottage of retired General Maximo Gomez in Santo Domingo. The old veteran, now seventy-two, at once joined the poet-liberator, declaring, "We will conquer and be free, cost what it may, or happen what will, though we have to raise a hospital on each corner and a tomb in each home."

On April 10, 1895, on a black and stormy night, José Martí, General Maximo Gomez, and their followers reached Cuba. It was the first time in sixteen years that the poet-liberator had stood on Cuban soil. Together the two heroes of the Cuban people dropped to their knees in the sand and prayed.

Six weeks later, Martí was dead. Betrayed by a guide, he was shot while on his white horse on May 19, 1895.

The pages that follow are the last two pages of the diary Martí kept to document the revolution.

On the March in Cuba, May 16, 1895: We set out, the whole force. Suddenly a group of horsemen. Maceo, on a bright day, in a suit of gray drill, silver-trimmed saddle, finely made and star-studded. He had come to look for us. The plantation received us like a festival. The delight and admiration of servants and workers is evident: the owner, a red-faced old man with side burns, panama hat, and small feet brings out vermouth, cigars, rum. "Kill three, five, ten, fourteen chickens." A woman in open-necked dress and house slippers comes to offer us green brandy with herbs in it. Crowds of people come and go. Maceo's aide, lively and talkative, keeps on the move. Maceo and Gomez talk in a low voice near me: in a little while they call me over to the entrance to the house. Night is falling over Cuba, and Maceo has to travel six hours. His troops are nearby, but he does not take us to see them.

Quick leave-taking on horseback. "You're going that way and we go on," and we go on, with a disgruntled escort, night falling, without orderlies, not sure of our way, to a shed on the road. We keep on to another muddy cabin, outside the camp, open to attack. General Gomez sends for meat and orderlies bring it. And thus, as though rejected, with sad thoughts, we sleep. The next day we leave Jagua, with its old, loyal fighters for freedom, for El Mijial. On the way we talk about the old war. . . .

We come straight into the Rio Savannah, a green expanse surrounded by woods, with palms. The dark paths through the green grass, sprinkled here and there with purple or white flowers. To the right, on the crest of the dense sierra, pines. It is raining hard. . . . To the sound of bugles we reach the ranch . . . we enter the cabin on horseback because it is too muddy outside for us to dismount, there is a stench from the mud and the air because of the many cattle that have died nearby. The low cabin is slung with hammocks. In a corner, on a stove, kettles bubble. They bring us coffee, ginger water, and an infusion of guanabana leaves.

Garcia was there, on that hill, the whole hill was nothing but Cubans. And on the other side there was another force.

The breast swells with fond reverence and overpowering affection at the sight of the vast landscape, of the loved river. We cross it. And after greeting a patriot family, overjoyed to see us, we enter the open wood, with sweet sun, rain-washed leaves. Over a carpet go our horses, so thick with the grass. All is garland and leaf, and through the openings, the green of the cleared fields is visible on the other bank, sheltered and compact.

Here as everywhere I am touched by the affection with which we are received, and the unity of soul which will not be allowed to coalesce, and which will not be recognized and which will be overridden, harming at least with the harm of delay, the revolution in the impulse of its first year. The spirit I sowed is that which has borne fruit and that of the island, and with it, and guarding ourselves by it, we will soon triumph, and with a better victory and for a better peace. I foresee that, for a time at least, the force of the revolution will be divorced from the spirit, deprived of the charm and pleasure and the power of victory of this natural association.

All the troops since my entry in the camp have called me President. And at each camp I come to, the respect surges up, and a certain warm enthusiasm of general affection, and evidence of the pleasure of the people in my presence and simplicity.

I suddenly see the Cauto [river], now full with wide bed in the hollow of the ravines on either side. And there came to my mind, at the sight of such beauty, the thought of man's low, fierce passions. As we approached, a man was roping a heifer, black with budding horns, and holding her against a tree; the horses, heads high, snorted. Their eyes gleamed.

Night rain, mud, bath in the Contramaestre [river]; the caress of running water, the silk of the water. In the afternoon a messenger: Maceo is in Sabana, looking for us. They bring a supply wagon captured in La Ratonera. They empty it at the door; Bellito divides it up; there's cloth, which Bellito measured out by armlengths, so much for the escort, so much for Pacheco, the captain of the convoy, and Bellito's men, so much for the General Staff; candles, a length of goods for Rosario's wife, onions, garlic, and potatoes and olives for Valentin.

Gomez sets out with forty horsemen to harry the supply train of Bayamo. I remain writing with the help of Garriga and Feria, who copy the *General Instruc-*

tions for commanders and officers; with twelve men, under Lieutenant Chacon, with three pickets at the three roads; and beside me, Graziano Perez, Rosario, on his pony, with mud to the knees, affectionately brings me lunch in his knapsack: "I'd give my life for you." From Santiago, which they recently left, come the brothers Chacon, one of whom captured the string of horses day before yesterday, and his brother, fair, pedantic, comical, and José Cabrera, the shoemaker of Jiguaní, stuttering and frank, and Duane, black, young, and . . . Avalos, timid, and Rafael Vazques, and Desiderio Soler, sixteen years old, whom Charles treats like a son. There is another son here, Ezequiel Morales, eighteen years old, whose father was killed in the wars. And those who come to tell me about Rosa Moreno, the country widow, who sent her only son Melesio, sixteen, to Rabi: "Your father died there; I can't go anymore; you go." They roast plantains, and pound dried beef soft with a stone in the mortar for the recent arrivals. The floodwaters of the Contramaestre are very roiled, and Valentin brings me a pitcher of boiled water, sweetened with higo leaves.

I wish to leave the world
By its natural door;
In my tomb of green leaves
They are to carry me to die,
Do not put me in the dark
To die like a traitor
I am good: like a good being
I will die with my face in the sun.
Man cannot be more perfect than the sun.
The sun burns with the same ray that warms.
The sun has spots. The unfortunate speak only
of the spots. The fortunate speak of the light.

José Martí

ADDRESS TO THE PEOPLE OF THE UNITED STATES

BY

TOMAS ESTRADA PALMA[9]

Tomás Estrada Palma—Cuban patriot, freedom fighter, and the first president of the Republic of Cuba, elected in 1902—was exiled for years in the United States. He opened a school for boys in Orange County, New York, but fellow Cubans were fighting for their freedom from Spain, and the exiled Estrada Palma was soon working for the rebel cause. José Martí, fellow patriot in exile and head of the Cuban junta in New York, visited Estrada Palma, and for some years they worked together to further the cause of Cuban freedom, raising money and speaking to Cubans living in the United States.

Soon after Martí's death in May 1895, Estrada Palma addressed the people of the United States, comparing the cause of the Cuban patriots in their war against Spain to that of the rebels in the Revolutionary War waged by the thirteen colonies against the British government after 1776.

To the People of the United States: The persistency with which the American press has, during the last few years, been treating proposed administrative reforms to be introduced in Cuba by the government of Spain compels me to request the publication of the following declaration which I make in behalf of my government, of the Army of Liberation of Cuba, and of the Cuban Revolutionary party.

If Spain has power to exterminate us, then let her

After the death of his mother at the hands of the Spaniards, Tomás Estrada Palma devoted his life to freeing Cuba from Spanish rule. He became the Republic of Cuba's first president in 1902.

convert the island into a vast cemetery; if she has not, and wishes to terminate the war before the whole country is reduced to ashes, then let her adopt the only measure that would put an end to it and recognize our independence. Spain must know by this time that while there is a single Cuban with dignity—and there are many thousands of them—here will be no peace in Cuba, nor even hope of it.

All good causes must finally triumph and ours is a good cause. It is the cause of justice treated with contempt, of right suppressed by force, and of the dignity of the people offended to the last degree.

We Cubans have a thousandfold more reasons in our endeavors to free ourselves from the Spanish yoke than the people of the thirteen colonies had when, in 1776, they rose in arms against the British government.

The people of these colonies were in full enjoyment of all the rights of man; they had liberty and conscience, freedom of speech, liberty of the press, the right of public meeting, and the right of free locomotion; they elected those who governed them, they made their own laws and, in fact, enjoyed the blessings of self-government. They were not under the sway of a captain-general with arbitrary powers who at his will could imprison them, deport them to penal colonies, or to order their execution, even without the semblance of a court-martial. They did not have to pay a permanent army and navy that they might be kept in subjection nor to feed a swarm of hungry employees yearly sent over from the metropolis to prey upon the country.

They were never subjected to a stupid and crushing customs tariff which compelled them to go to the home markets for millions [of dollars' worth] of merchandise annually which they could buy much cheaper elsewhere; they were never compelled to accept a budget of $26 million or $30 million a year without the consent of the taxpayers, and for the purpose of defraying the expenses of the army and navy of the oppressor, to pay the salaries of thousands of worthless European employees, the whole interest on a debt not incurred by the colony, and other expenditures from which the island received no benefit whatever; for out of all these millions, only the paltry sum of $700,000 was apparently applied for works of internal improvement, one half of which invariably went into the pockets of the Spanish employees.

We have thrown ourselves into the struggle advisedly and deliberately; we knew what we would have to face, and we decided unflinchingly to persevere until we should emancipate ourselves from the Spanish government. And we know that we are able to do it, as we know that we are competent to govern ourselves.

The war in Cuba has for its only object the overthrow of Spanish power and to establish an independent republic, under whose beneficent laws the Spaniards may continue to live side by side with the Cubans as members of the same community and citizens of the same nation. This is our program, and we strictly adhere to it.

The revolution is powerful and deeply rooted in the hearts of the Cuban people, and there is no Spanish power—no power in the world—that can stop its march. The war, since General Weyler took command of the Spanish army, has assumed a cruel character; his troops shoot the Cuban prisoners, pursue and kill the sick and wounded, assassinate the unarmed, and burn their houses. The Cuban troops, on their part, destroy, as a war measure, the machinery and buildings of the sugar plantations and are firmly resolved not to leave one stone upon another during their campaign.

Let those who can put an end to this war reflect that our liberty is being gained with the thousands of Cuban victims, among whom is numbered José Martí, the apostle and martyr of our revolution. Let them consider that, before the sacred memory of this new redeemer, there is not a single Cuban who will withdraw from the work of emancipation without feeling ashamed of abandoning the flag which, on the twenty-fourth of February, was raised by the beloved master.

It is time for the Cuban people to satisfy their just

desire for a place among the free nations of the world, and let them not be accused if to accomplish their noble purpose they are obliged to reduce to ashes the Cuban land.

THE LAST SKIRMISH
IN LAS VILLAS
BY GROVER FLINT[10]

In 1895 war broke out once again between Cuba and Spain. The Spanish government in Cuba had become increasingly corrupt and tyrannical, spurring Cuban patriots to revolt. Spain sent 200,000 fresh troops to support its cause and defend its rule. But the much smaller army of patriots under General Maximo Gomez engaged the Spanish soldiers in guerrilla warfare. Able to move quickly from place to place, and capable of living off the land, the guerrillas avoided large battles against what would have been overwhelming odds. That way they were able to win ultimate victory.

Grover Flint, a young and adventurous American, traveled to Cuba in 1896. His objective was to collect firsthand information on the true state of affairs in Cuba. He decided to visit the insurgent patriots to see for himself how things were actually going in this new war for Cuban independence.

The excerpt that follows tells of Flint's experience. He swore that his report was the "plain, unvarnished" truth about what he had seen and heard.

Gomez had his last skirmish for that season in Las Villas. A large force of Spaniards had arrived in the neighborhood and were in camp two miles away. From midnight on, there was shooting, for Gomez promptly sent a party of local infantry to keep the gringos awake. By daybreak . . . the firing was nearer. The infantry was retreating in our direction, and the troops had turned out and were following. By six o'clock, our camp guards were engaged, and the impedimenta was already retreating into the mountains of the Grupo Cubanacan. The retreat led through . . . hilly country, thickly wooded, with here and there pastures, within stone walls. The Spaniards advanced more swiftly than I had ever seen them. Instead of keeping to the roads as usual, they swarmed into the woods, blazing away through the underbrush, pushing our men back by weight of numbers alone, over rugged hills and stone walls until they were on the very heels of the impedimenta [supply carriers] and still within hand-shaking distance of the enemy. Gomez was angry and blamed the guide, who had led us by a bad way. Three hours of pursuit had not lessened the ardor of the regulars. Few of Gomez's officers had seen anything like it since the war began. At last a rocky hill rose before us, and an open patch wound over it corkscrew fashion, in plain view from below. Here there was trouble with impedimenta. They were exposed to a fire that drove over our heads and pattered amongst them like hail.

One of the impedimenta was shot and fell with his horse directly in the narrowest part of the way, and it took several minutes to get him out. To hurry matters, the impedimenta, as it reached the summit, split into three parties, making off, for the sake of speed, in different directions over the brow of the hill.

Then the road was clear, and it was the turn of the staff, and the rear guard, Guerra's men, to go up.

Gomez led, and there was scrambling and swearing and lashing of horses, as the staff and rear guard followed, jostling one another. If a horse fell, a man jerked off the saddle and bridle as quickly as he could to beat the crouching animal, with drawn machete, out of the pathway. When a man lay down and called for help, volunteers dismounted, took him on their shoulders or on their horses, and hurried him along.

I observed no unnecessary delay, even on the part of the reckless Gutiérrez, who rode just in front of me, digging his heels into the horse's flank and looking straight ahead, and the cavalry drillmaster's "four feet from the head to croup" was forgotten.

At the top, Gomez paused and gave old Ramón Guerra orders not to let the Spanish up, even if he had to hold them back with machetes. When the last of the rear guard had joined us, the trail was open, a sunny glistening path, encumbered by four dead horses. One horse that had fallen, scrambled to his feet, goaded by flying pebbles and ricochet bullets, and came limping with drooping head up the trail after us.

The Spaniards did not try that pass, and our retreat became more dignified. Seven troopers were reported severely wounded, and three dead men were being carried, slung on lead horses.

The insurgents never desert their wounded. It is part of their religion to stay with them. I have never seen or heard, on good evidence, an exception to this rule. As Gomez says, "The wounded are sacred."

The impedimenta was signaled to halt, and from it stout Negroes were detailed to carry the helpless. Hammocks were borrowed from those who had them to lend, and the wounded were borne in them, slung on poles on the shoulders of their comrades. Two men carried a pole for a hundred yards or so, and rested it on crotched sticks that they drove upright in the ground at each halt, while they caught their wind and mopped their sweaty brows. A third man shouldered those crotched sticks and changed places with the first pole-bearer who gave out.

Nine more were wounded, but able to take care of

themselves; among them General Vega, Gomez's chief of staff, received a ricochet ball in the ankle that took in a bit of his leather legging with it, and bothered him for many weeks afterward.

We moved slowly, supposing the Spaniards far behind. The impedimenta had disappeared among the hills and the staff carelessly jogged along with the last files of the rear guard. On a bluff overlooking the country was a cottage, and from its door a middle-aged woman with three small children gazed at us, trembling, for they had heard the approaching roar of musketry. We dismounted to reconnoiter with field glasses. Fully one thousand yards back, through an open spot on the opposite hillside, we could see Spanish infantry straggling in another direction, and an officer on a white horse was looking back at us through his field glasses.

It was already eleven o'clock, and we stood in a bunch, passing the glass from one to another. Gomez was prominent in the foreground. Suddenly, from the leafy vale bellow, the barking of Mausers. A detachment of Spaniards had come upon us by another trail and were shooting at close range, not two hundred yards away. The soldiers had begun firing as they came up. Had they waited until enough were together to send a good wound volley, they might have got more of us, even our commander in chief, but we did not wait for volleys. We lost no time in mounting and hurrying after the rear guard, leaving the mother and children screaming, "*Ay, Dios mio!*" in each other's arms; for the gringos were coming and they knew not which way to run. They were the last shots that day. A mile further on we halted. Deep in the woods, some distance from the road, a camp was made for the wounded, and the dead were buried. Graves were dug with poles made from saplings sharpened to a point with machetes. The equipment was removed from the dead and apportioned among those who needed [it] most. A man tried on the hat, leggings, and shoes of his late comrade as he lay on the ground and kept them if a fit, or if not, passed them to his neighbor; for in the field, it is so difficult to get clothing of any kind.

From our point of view, the day was a victory because two columns, acting in combination, had chased us as a brace of hounds chases a hare, and failed to bag us all. Yet, our loss, twenty wounded and three killed outright, nearly all on the open hillside where the impedimenta came under fire, was far greater than usual in such skirmishes.

Early that afternoon, we were resting in a peaceful camp, on a branch of the river, near the pasture of Palo Prieto, and the toll of the morning, with its loss of life and blood, was already forgotten.

GENERAL MAXIMO GOMEZ
BY GROVER FLINT[11]

He is a gray little man. His clothes do not fit well, and perhaps, if you saw it in a photograph, his figure might seem old and ordinary. The moment he turns his keen eyes on you, they strike like a blow from the shoulder. You feel the will, the fearlessness, and the experience of men that is in those eyes, and their owner becomes a giant before you.

He is a farmer by birth, the son of a farmer, with an Anglo-Saxon tenacity of purpose, and a sense of honor as clean and true as the blade of his little Santo Domingo machete.

When the revolution broke out in Santo Domingo, he served as lieutenant in the Spanish army against the land of his birth, in her struggle for independence. He was fighting for rank, I've heard him say, but the example of the Dominican patriots, and the methods of his brother soldiers, made him think. In later years, he came to believe with the Cubans that Cuba should be free, and when others dared only whisper, he proclaimed his sympathies, and was relieved of a captain's commission in consequence.

"THE DEATH OF GENERAL ANTONIO MACEO" BY GONZALO DE QUESADA[12]

Antonio Maceo, the son of Marcos Maceo, a mulatto cattle driver, was one of the heroic military figures of the Cuban wars for independence. Born in Santiago de Cuba on July 14, 1848, he was a strong young man, a cattle driver like his father. When war erupted, Marcos Maceo, whose house had been burned and whose family had been brutalized by the Spaniards, gathered his children and stepchildren around him, and all of them together took a solemn oath to fight to the end for Cuba's freedom from Spanish rule. Ultimately, Antonio and thirteen of his brothers gave their lives in the cause of liberty.

In the first battle he took part in, Antonio Maceo so distinguished himself that he was personally congratulated by his general. Without favoritism or help from outside, Antonio rose by sheer brilliance and fearlessness to the highest rank in the Cuban army. For ten years he fought in battle after battle, always at the head of his troops, until finally his life was cut short by treachery.

Although his army was constantly outnumbered by the Spanish forces, Maceo's superb generalship was so astonishing that his exploits captured worldwide attention. He died on the battlefield just as he was about to launch a daring campaign against Spanish domination with an attack on the suburbs of Havana.

With him died Francisco Gomez, the young son of his comrade-in-arms, the great Maximo Gomez. Francisco's body lay close beside that of his leader, and a letter, written in pencil, and addressed to his family, was attached to his body.

Dear Mamma, Papa, Dear Brothers; I die at my post. I did not want to abandon the body of General Maceo, and I stayed with him. I was wounded in two places, and as I did not want to fall into the hands of the enemy I have killed myself. I am dying. I die pleased at dying in the defense of the Cuban cause. I wait for you in the other world.

Your son, Francisco Gomez

Torro [Village] in San Domingo
(Friends or foes, please transmit this to its destination as requested by one who's dead.)

December 7, 1896: There is one dark day that will forever be remembered by the Cubans. On that day fell Antonio Maceo. The life of the hero was cut short by treachery in the moment in which he was to astonish the world by a most brilliant blow to Spanish domination, an attack on the suburbs of Havana.

General Maceo was marching with his men on

[December 7] when they met Major Cirujeda with six hundred of the San Quintín regiment, famous for its killing of Pacíficos. At first General Maceo took them to be Cubans; soon the error was discovered. A fierce battle followed, General Maceo commanding the center; the outlook was so bright that General Maceo exclaimed, "This goes well." To decide the engagement, he charged, his machete on high, at the head of his staff, as he had done a hundred times before. Fifty paces from the enemy a terrific volley laid him low, with the valiant Francisco Gomez, the son of the general-in-chief. Only General Miró escaped wounded.

The Spaniards, defeated, were forced to retreat to Punta Brava; the Cubans recovered the body, which they secretly buried. Thus died the wonderful mulatto, the most illustrious, perhaps, of his race. His public life was consecrated to liberty; he knew no vice or mean action; he would not permit any around him. When he landed, he was told there were no arms. "I will get them with my machete," he answered, and he left five thousand to his country, conquered by the power of his arm.

He was modest. When some young flatterer told him: "You are by right the general-in-chief, because you were the last to surrender in the last war," he replied, "My sword can never compare with that of General Maximo Gomez." He was a man of lofty ideals: when the Spanish press propagated the calumny that he was aiming at a colored republic, he sent me word to then and always assert over my signature: "General Maceo is neither black nor white; he is a Cuban." That is the man, a Cuban, and for that reason it is fitting that General Miró should have saturated his handkerchief with the blood of the patriot, so that he could show it to his countrymen as the symbol of sacrifice, and that it may serve to keep them alive to their duty of dying like the hero, Antonio Maceo, who never surrendered to the Spanish tyranny.

"THE FATE OF THE PACIFICOS" BY RICHARD HARDING DAVIS[13]

When General Valeriano Weyler was sent to Cuba to take command of the Spanish forces there, he arrived with a reputation for cruelty which he had earned during the Ten Years' War. Before long, he had not only lived up to his advance publicity, but had behaved so brutally that he became known throughout the world as "Butcher Weyler."

His most outrageous innovation was known as his "reconcentrado policy." This meant that all Cubans—men, women, and children—were ordered to move into fortified towns watched over by Spanish troops. No civilian was allowed to enter the reconcentrados without a passport, under penalty of death and forfeiture of property. Crowded into these concentration camps, with nothing to do, with no provisions to keep them alive, and with no medical care, the unfortunate people died by the thousands. In the province of La Habana alone, 52,000 men, women and children died.

In the excerpt that follows, Richard Harding Davis, an American war correspondent, describes his visit to a typical camp and quotes General Weyler's own defiant description of himself: "I care not for America, England, or anyone, but only for the treaties we have with them. They are the law. I know I am merciless, but mercy has no place in war. I care not what is said about me. I am not a politician. I am Weyler."

Traveling with Richard Harding Davis was the American painter and sculptor Frederic Remington, who was covering the war for the Hearst papers. He gives us his personal picture of "Butcher Weyler": "A little man. An apparition of black—black eyes, black hair, black beard—dark, exceedingly dark complexion—a plain black attire, black shoes, black tie, and soiled standing collar and not a relief from the aspect of darkness anywhere on his person."

As is already well known in the United States, General Weyler issued an order some months ago commanding the country people living in the provinces of Pinar del Rio, La Habana, and Matanzas to betake themselves with their belongings to the fortified towns. His object in doing this was to prevent the pacíficos [country people] from giving help to the insurgents and from sheltering them and the wounded in their huts. So flying columns of guerrillas and Spanish soldiers were sent to burn these huts and to drive the inhabitants into the suburbs of the cities. When I arrived in Cuba, sufficient time had passed for me to note the effects of this order and to study the results as they are to be found in the provinces of La Habana, Matanzas, and Santa Clara, the order having been extended to embrace the latter provinces.

It looked then as if General Weyler was reaping what he had sown and was face to face with a problem of his own creation. As far as a visitor could judge, the results of the famous order seemed to furnish a better argument to those who think the United States should interfere on behalf of Cuba, than did the fact that men are being killed there and that both sides were devastating the island and wrecking property worth millions of dollars.

The order proved an exceedingly shortsighted one and acted almost immediately after the manner of a boomerang. The able-bodied men of each family who had remained loyal or at least neutral, so long as they were permitted to live undisturbed on their few acres, were not content to exist on the charity of the city, and swarmed over to the insurgent ranks by the hundreds, and it was only the old and infirm and the women and children who went into the towns, where they at once became a burden on the Spanish residents, who were already distressed by the lack of trade and the high prices asked for food.

The order failed also in its original object of embarrassing the insurgents, for they are used to living out of doors and finding food for themselves, and the destruction of the huts where they had been made welcome was not a great loss to men who, in a few minutes, with the aid of machete, can construct a shelter from a palm tree.

So the order failed to distress those against whom it was aimed, but brought swift and terrible suffering to those who were and are absolutely innocent of any intent against the government, as well as to the adherents of the government.

It is easy to imagine what happened when hundreds of people, in some towns thousands, were herded together on the bare ground with no food and no knowledge of sanitation, with no covering for their heads but palm leaves, with no privacy for the women and young girls, with no thought but of how they could live until tomorrow.

It is true that in the country also these people had no covering for their huts but palm leaves, but those huts were made stoutly to endure. When a man built one of them, he was building his home, not a shelter tent, and they were placed well apart from one another with the free air of the plain or mountain blowing about them. The huts in which these people live at present lean one against the other, and there are no broad roads, no green tobacco patches, to separate one from another. They are, on the contrary, only narrow paths, two feet wide, where dogs and cattle and human beings tramp daily over growing heaps of refuse and garbage and filth, and where malaria rises at night in a white sheet of poisonous mist.

In Jaruco, in La Habana Province, a town of only two thousand inhabitants, the deaths from smallpox averaged seven a day for the month of December, and while Frederic Remington and I were there, six victims of smallpox were carried up the hill to the burying ground in the space of twelve hours. There were Spanish soldiers, as well as *pacíficos* among these, for the Spanish officers neither care or know anything about the health of their men.

Around every town and even around the forts outside the towns, you will see from one hundred to five hundred of these palm huts, with the people crouched about them, covered with rags, starving, with no chance to obtain work.

The warehouses in Cárdenas, one of the principal seaport towns, are built on wooden posts about fifty feet from the water's edge. Some time ago, an unusually high tide swept in under one of the warehouses and left a pool of water a hundred yards long around the wooden posts, and it has remained there undisturbed. This pool is covered a half inch thick with green slime, with the damp fungus spread over the wooden posts.

Over this sewage are now living three hundred women and children and a few men. The floor beneath them is rotted away, and the planks are broken and have fallen into the pool, leaving big gaps, through which rise day and night deadly stenches and poisonous exhalations from the pool below.

One gentleman of Cárdenas told me that a hundred of these people called at his house every day for food.

I found the hospital for this colony behind three blankets which had been hung across a counter of the warehouse. A young woman and a man were lying side by side; the others sat within a few feet of them on the other side of the blanket, apparently lost to all sense of their danger, and even too dejected and hopeless to raise their eyes when I gave them money. I asked the doctor what ailed the patients, and he said it was yellow fever and pointed again at the slime, which moved and bubbled in the hot sun. He showed me the babies with skin drawn so tightly over their little bodies that their bones showed through. They were covered with sores, and they protested as loudly as they could, clenching their fists and sobbing with pain when the sore places came in contact with their mother's arms.

A gentleman told me that in the huts at the back of the town there had been twenty-five cases of smallpox in one week, in which seventeen had resulted in death.

In other wars, men have fought with men, and women have suffered indirectly because the men were killed. But in this war, it is the women, herded together in the towns like cattle, who are going to die, while men, camped in the fields and the mountains, will live.

THE SINKING OF THE TILLIS BY DYNAMITE JOHNNY O'BRIEN, WITH HORACE SMITH[14]

"Dynamite" Johnny O'Brien was a daring blockade-runner during Cuba's long struggle to free herself from Spanish rule. The ammunition so crucial to the patriots' cause reached its destination in great part due to O'Brien's courageous efforts.

Born of Irish parents in a tenement on New York's East Side, Dynamite Johnny lived a life packed with daring adventures before he died on March 27, 1917. His last wish, expressed to Victor H. Barranco, then a Cuban consular official in New York, was to be buried in the sailors' cemetery at City Island, "as near the water's edge as possible." His wish was fulfilled, but his grave, three feet above the high-water mark, had no tombstone. The *Times* of Cuba, hearing of this and remembering the vital part Dynamite Johnny had played in bringing ammunition to the Cuban patriots, raised a fund by public subscription to erect a granite monument at his grave.

In the excerpt that follows, written in 1897, Johnny O'Brien tells the exciting story of one of his more desperate adventures in filibustering. Incidentally, he gives us an interesting sidelight on the infamous de Lôme letter that was to play so prominent a role in President William McKinley's decision to take the United States into a war with Spain.

Throughout my career as a filibuster [an irregular military adventurer] with all of the close shaves that go with persistence in that profession, I commanded but one expedition on which there was any loss of life; that was the tragic trip of the *Tillis*. The *Tillis* was an old steamer that had been carrying freight between New York and New London, Connecticut, for a New England railroad. While undergoing repairs, she was offered for sale at a bargain, and after I had pronounced her hull in good condition, and Frank Pagluchi had inspected and passed her machinery, the Cubans bought her.

Her purchase was dictated by a desire to land a large shipment of munitions of war in Cuba as quickly as possible, to offset the capital the Spaniards were trying to make out of the death of Lieutenant-General Antonio Maceo, who was killed on December 7, 1896, as he was leading a detachment of troops against Havana. He had planned a quick, sharp raid on the capital to give the lie to General Blanco, who was loudly proclaiming that he had Maceo bottled up in Pinar del Rio and that the revolt had finally been stamped out. When it was discovered that the most dashing of the rebel leaders had been put out of commission, there was great rejoicing at Havana and Madrid, and General Blanco blatantly boasted that with [Maceo's] death, the rebellion was actually at an end. It was feared that this might be believed, and we wished to prove to our American sympathizers that there was no thought of giving up the fight.

In the hurry of getting the *Tillis* away, the men who were overhauling her neglected to take out the tail shaft, which was a fatal mistake, though that was the last place one would look for a break. With her repairs completed, as was supposed, Captain George W. Berry took her around to the easterly end of Long Island, with instructions to lie to between Montauk Point and Gardiners Island, ten miles inside of the lighthouse. While the steamer was being repaired, the sleuths became suspicious that we were planning another expedition, though they had no clue as to what we were doing, and the force of detectives which constantly watched my home and trailed me every time I left the house, was doubled. They had been fooled so often that they were on the alert every minute, and I had feared that I might have some trouble eluding them; but a happy coincidence made it easy.

The thirtieth anniversary of my marriage fell on Friday, January 21, and the neighbors, without any idea that they were aiding my plans, arranged to celebrate the event that evening. It was to be a surprise party for Mrs. O'Brien, who was over in Brooklyn to get her out of the way, and late in the afternoon thirty or forty of her friends took charge of things and proceeded to decorate the house. The detectives, who knew what was going on, did not imagine that I would leave at such a time, so they accommodatingly relaxed their vigilance. As soon as it was dark, without even waiting for Mrs. O'Brien to come home, I slipped out by the back way and hurried over to New York, where Dr. Castillo, Cartaya, and a party of Cuban officers were waiting for me on a tug. We at once put off through the Sound and reached the *Tillis* on Saturday morning.

The two tugs, towing two large lighters loaded with arms, arrived from Bridgeport at the same time. They had started for New York, according to the report that was given out, and the detectives were waiting for them there. The particular pride of this expedition was a beautiful dynamite gun, which had been on exhibition in New York and was considered the most destructive weapon in the world as well as the most terrifying. To keep it company, there were three million cartridges, several thousand machetes, and a lot of small arms and medical supplies. It was a cargo well calculated to arouse enthusiasm among the rebels and enable them to operate more effectively and offensively.

With a lighter at each side, the *Tillis* was loaded in about six hours, and we put to sea late in the afternoon, heading east southeast to keep well clear of the shore and prevent them from getting our direction from the lighthouse, where the ship was so well known that she would have been recognized at a glance. There was a revenue cutter lying at New London, and we feared she would try to pick up our trail as soon as the patient detectives discovered that the arms which they were expecting in New York had taken another course. During the night the *Tillis* began to leak, but the chief engineer failed to notify me as he should have done. It was this theory, he claimed, that as the vessel had been in dry dock long enough to get thoroughly dried out, the strain of her cargo had opened up some of her seams, and he supposed they would tighten up as soon as her timbers expanded under the action of the water, and that until then the pumps could handle the leakage. But the water did not seep in through started seams; it poured in through the sleeve of the tail shaft.

When I discovered on Sunday morning that something was wrong, the water was over the shaft, and it was too late to make any investigation; besides there were other things of more importance to be done, for even then the water was beginning to splash the fires out. The pumps were losing ground every minute, and it was plain enough that the ship was bound for the bottom of the sea; it was only a question of whether she sank in deep or shallow water. I immediately hauled her around and headed for Long Island in the hope that we could keep her going until I could run her ashore. It was then blowing hard from the southeast, so we had the wind with us to start with; but from the looks of things, I knew it would be only a few hours until we ran into a northwester.

In an effort to keep the fires above the rapidly rising water, I ordered the cargo thrown overboard. When I thought how much the Spanish minister in Washington would have enjoyed seeing the bundles of rifles and boxes of cartridges send up bubbles, I fervently wished we had him on board—but not for that reason alone. The wonderful dynamite gun, in which so many hopes had been centered, was held until the last, and when it went overboard, I turned my back; I could not bear to see it go. In spite of all we could do to lighten the ship, the water gained on us. When it finally put out the fires, we kept some steam up for a while by burning waste soaked in oil, but by noon, when we were within a few miles of the shore, the water was so far above the grate bars that it was impossible to keep anything alight under the boilers. After that, it was simply a case of trusting to Providence.

About the time the last little fire was snuffed out, the wind backed around into the northwest and blew us straight out to sea. The change in wind dismissed any thought we might have had of taking to the boats, though in the sea that was running, it would have been a miracle if they had [lasted] long enough to carry us halfway to the shore. In half an hour it was blowing a living gale, and bitter cold. Every few minutes a big comber swept the helpless ship from stem to stern, and our clothes were so stiff that holes were broken in them as we moved around to keep from freezing to death. Captain Berry, who should have set an example to his crew, added to the strain on our taut nerves by continually whining like a baby.

"What is the matter with you, anyway?" I asked him, after he had made an exhibition of himself that set some of the others to weeping.

"I've got a wife and two children at home," he blubbered.

"Then I'm three times worse off than you are," I told him, "for I've got the best wife in the world and eight children. It looks as if they are going to have to get along without me from this time on, but crying isn't going to help them, and it certainly won't do me any good. They would be ashamed of me if they thought I showed myself a coward. Try to be a man for a change; you'll feel better about it."

We looked in vain for another craft of any kind, and by the middle of the afternoon it seemed as though it was all up with us, for there was not much daylight left, and with her deck almost awash, it was impossible that the *Tillis* could keep afloat all night. The gale had swept us out to sea so rapidly that by that time we were fifteen miles offshore. The wind, which was filled with icy needles, had kicked up a wild cross-sea and it was more comfortable to go down with the ship than to even think of trying to escape in the boats.

Just as I had practically given up hope, the *Governor Ames* hove in sight, tearing up the coast to windward of us under double-reefed lower sails. I have always been partial to windjammers and have seen many that aroused my admiration, but the *Ames* impressed me by all odds as the most beautiful ship I had ever seen.

There probably would have been two wrecks instead of one if she had tried to get a close quarters with us, so it was necessary for us to take to the boats and get well clear of the *Tillis* before we could get picked up.

A line was thrown to us, but the Cuban who caught it was unable to hold it. I jumped and caught it, took a turn around a thwart, and it held. Then we made ropes fast to ourselves and were hauled aboard. Most of us had to be lifted over the rail and fell on the deck almost senseless from complete exhaustion.

Good news sometimes follows on the heels of bad, and within a few days after the *Tillis* went down, Mr. Palma [Tomás Estrada Palma, a leader in the Cuban resistance movement and the first president of a free Cuba] received word through one of our secret channels that a messenger was on his way to New York with an important document which he would be able to use to great advantage. When the anxiously awaited Cuban arrived, it developed that he bore a letter written by Dupuy de Lôme, the Spanish minister at Washington, to a friend in Havana, in which he spoke of President McKinley as a "low politician." This document, which had fallen into the hands of the Cubans in a manner that made it appear to be a gift from the gods, was rightly regarded as more valuable ammunition than shiploads of dynamite or carloads of guns, for it required no prophetic vision to discern the effect its publication would produce.

First and foremost, it assured us of more kindly consideration at the one Spanish stronghold on which we had been unable to make any impression—the White House at Washington. Instead of having "catered to the rabble," as was charged by de Lôme, Mr. McKinley had maintained an attitude that was absolutely correct from the standpoint of international law, though extremely incorrect, as I believed, for the president of the greatest republic on earth. He had never evinced the slightest sympathy for the Cubans in public or private and had exerted all of the forces at his command to prevent assistance from reaching them. To influential members of his own party who had urged him to intervene in Cuba, to put an end to wholesale murder and countless Spanish brutalities within sight of the American flag, he had repeatedly declared that he "would not be forced into an unholy war." [Since McKinley had] taken such a dedicated stand against the growing sentiment of his country, we knew the vulgar criticism of de Lôme would deeply wound his pride, which is a vulnerable point with most men, even though they are strong enough to be moved in no other way.

It was equally easy to foresee the effect of this momentous communication on the general public. Behind their patriotic impulses, the people of all parties felt a personal affection for McKinley that has been shown to few presidents, and whether or not they agreed with his pro-Spanish policy, they would never stand to have him abused by the diplomatic representative of any European power, and least of all by the minister from Spain. We all believed the letter would result in the anticipated American intervention, as it undoubtedly would have done if the blowing up of the *Maine*, which quickly followed, had not given the

United States a much stronger though less valid reason for anger. The de Lôme document was made public on February 9, and it produced the expected effect; but before popular indignation had time to crystallize, the incident was forgotten in the excitement over the calamity at Havana.

When we resumed the fight for Cuba, it was with the American flag flying over us, and under it we found situations as stirring as any we had experienced when we were operating in defiance of a tyrannical law and without any recognized flag. Strange as it may seem, I could see no difference, for the real principle involved seemed to me to have undergone no change.

A LETTER TO A FRIEND FROM THE SPANISH MINISTER, ENRIQUE DUPUY DE LOME[15]

During 1897, when the brutal policies employed by Spanish general Valeriano Weyler were reported in the United States press, the American public began to express sympathy for the Cuban population. In his annual message to Congress, President William McKinley criticized Spain harshly but stopped short of intervention. After reciting a number of reasons for American concern, including Cuba's close proximity to the United States, and America's investment of $30 million to $50 million in Cuban businesses—a sum whose value reached $103 million in 1893 and $96 million in 1894—he went on to say:

When the inability of Spain to deal successfully with the insurrection has become manifest, and it is demonstrated that her sovereignty is extinct in Cuba for all purposes of its rightful existence, and when a hopeless struggle for its reestablishment has degenerated into a strife which means nothing more than the useless sacrifice of human life and the utter destruction of the very subject matter of the conflict, a situation will be presented in which our obligations to the sovereignty of Spain will be superseded by higher obligations, which we can hardly hesitate to recognize and discharge.

During 1897 the American press attacked General Weyler continuously for his cruelty. Spain, too, was roundly denounced for its harsh policies. The American people were united in their sympathy for the Cuban insurgents. The Red Cross collected large sums to provide relief for the victims of Weyler's reconcentrado policy.

Said President McKinley: "It was not civilized warfare; it was extermination. The only peace it could beget is that of the wilderness and the grave."

In January 1898 the U.S. battleship *Maine* was ordered to Havana to protect the Americans in Cuba from the Spanish soldiers. Public resentment reached new heights when, only a week later, an indiscreet letter written to a friend by the Spanish minister in the United States, Dupuy de Lôme, fell into the hands of the Cubans, who sent it to the newspaper publisher, William Randolph·Hearst, who published it. In the letter Dupuy de Lôme used insulting language about President McKinley. A storm of criticism followed this disclosure, and Dupuy de Lôme, rather than risk recall, resigned at once.

The excitement had not yet subsided when on the 15th of February 1898, the *Maine* was mysteriously sunk in Havana harbor and 264 American sailors died.

When the people of the United States received news of the disaster, there was a great surge of patriotic feeling and a call went up from coast to coast: "Remember the *Maine!*"

. . . The President's [William McKinley's] message has undeceived the insurgents, who expected something else, and has paralyzed the action of Congress, but I consider it bad.

Besides the natural and inevitable coarseness with which he repeats all that the press and public opinion of Spain has said of Weyler, it shows once more what McKinley is—weak and catering to the rabble, and, besides, a low politician, who desires to leave a door open to me and to stand well with the jingoes of his party. Nevertheless, as a matter of fact, it will only depend on ourselves whether he will prove bad and adverse to us.

I agree entirely with you that without military and political success, there is here always danger that the insurgents will be encouraged, if not by the government, at least by part of the public opinion. I do not believe you pay enough attention to the role of England. Nearly all that newspaper canaille [riffraff], which swarm your hotel, are English and are correspondents of the best newspapers and reviews of London.

Thus it has been since the beginning. To my mind the only object of England is that Americans should occupy themselves with us and leave her in peace, and if there is a war, so much the better. That would further remove what is threatening her, although that will never happen. It would be most important that you should agitate the question of commercial relations, even though it would be only for effect, and that you should send here a man of importance, in order that I might use him to make propaganda among the senators and others, in opposition to the junta and to win over exiles.

Always your attentive friend and servant, who kisses your hands.

Enrique Dupuy de Lôme

THE YELLOW PRESS REPORTS OF THE SINKING OF THE MAINE FROM THE NEW YORK HERALD[16]

When the *Maine* was sunk, some American newspapers, known collectively as the Yellow Press, vied with each other in reporting the disaster. The excerpt that follows, taken from the *New York Herald*, is an example of the "Yellow Press."

The *Maine* Blown Up In Havana

February 15, 1898: Reports of a Terrific Explosion in the Harbor Which Totally Destroyed the Battleship

Many Persons Killed and Hurt
The Cruiser *Alfonso XII* and Other Spanish Vessels Aid in the Work of Rescuing the Crew

Explosion Shook the Whole City
Injured Members of the Crew Say They Were Asleep at the Time

Not Known How It Happened
Windows in All Parts of the Cuban Capital Shattered by the Terrible Concussion

Havana, Cuba, Tuesday—A terrible explosion took place on board the United States battleship *Maine* in Havana Harbor this evening at 10 o'clock.

Many were killed or wounded. All the boats of the Spanish cruiser *Alfonso XII* are assisting.

$50,000 REWARD.—WHO DESTROYED THE MAINE?—$50,000 REWARD.

EDITION FOR GREATER NEW YORK.

NEW YORK JOURNAL
AND ADVERTISER.

The Journal will give $50,000 for information, furnished to it exclusively, that will convict the person or persons who sank the Maine.

The Journal will give $50,000 for information, furnished to it exclusively, that will convict the person or persons who sank the Maine.

NO. 3,572. Copyright, 1898, by W. R. Hearst—NEW YORK, THURSDAY, FEBRUARY 17, 1898.—16 PAGES. PRICE ONE CENT in Greater New York. Two Cents elsewhere.

DESTRUCTION OF THE WAR SHIP MAINE WAS THE WORK OF AN ENEMY.

$50,000!
$50,000 REWARD!
For the Detection of the Perpetrator of the Maine Outrage!

The New York Journal hereby offers a reward of $50,000 CASH for information, FURNISHED TO IT EXCLUSIVELY, which shall lead to the detection and conviction of the person, persons or government criminally responsible for the explosion which resulted in the destruction, at Havana, of the United States war ship Maine and the loss of 258 lives of American sailors.

The $50,000 CASH offered for the above information is on deposit with Wells, Fargo & Co.

No one is barred, be he the humble but misguided seaman eking out a few miserable dollars by acting as a spy, or the attache of a government secret service, plotting, by any devilish means, to revenge financial insults or cripple menacing countries.

This offer has been cabled to Europe and will be made public in every capital of the Continent and in London this morning.

The Journal believes that any man who can be bought to commit murder can also be bought to betray his comrades. FOR THE PERPETRATOR OF THIS OUTRAGE HAD ACCOMPLICES.

W. R. HEARST.

Assistant Secretary Roosevelt Convinced the Explosion of the War Ship Was Not an Accident.

The Journal Offers $50,000 Reward for the Conviction of the Criminals Who Sent 258 American Sailors to Their Death. Naval Officers Unanimous That the Ship Was Destroyed on Purpose.

$50,000!
$50,000 REWARD!
For the Detection of the Perpetrator of the Maine Outrage!

The New York Journal hereby offers a reward of $50,000 CASH for information, FURNISHED TO IT EXCLUSIVELY, which shall lead to the detection and conviction of the person, persons or government criminally responsible for the explosion which resulted in the destruction, at Havana, of the United States war ship Maine and the loss of 258 lives of American sailors.

The $50,000 CASH offered for the above information is on deposit with Wells, Fargo & Co.

No one is barred, be he the humble but misguided seaman eking out a few miserable dollars by acting as a spy, or the attache of a government secret service, plotting, by any devilish means, to revenge financial insults or cripple menacing countries.

This offer has been cabled to Europe and will be made public in every capital of the Continent and in London this morning.

The Journal believes that any man who can be bought to commit murder can also be bought to betray his comrades. FOR THE PERPETRATOR OF THIS OUTRAGE HAD ACCOMPLICES.

W. R. HEARST.

POWDER MAGAZINE

NAVAL OFFICERS THINK THE MAINE WAS DESTROYED BY A SPANISH MINE.

George Eugene Bryson, the Journal's special correspondent at Havana, cables that it is the secret opinion of many Spaniards in the Cuban capital that the Maine was destroyed and 258 of her men killed by means of a submarine mine, or fixed torpedo. This is the opinion of several American naval authorities. The Spaniards, it is believed, arranged to have the Maine anchored over one of the harbor mines. Wires connected the mine with a powder magazine, and it is thought the explosion was caused by sending an electric current through the wire. If this can be proven, the brutal nature of the Spaniards will be shown by the fact that they waited to spring the mine until after all the men had retired for the night. The Maltese cross in the picture shows where the mine may have been fired.

Hidden Mine or a Sunken Torpedo Believed to Have Been the Weapon Used Against the American Man-of-War---Officers and Men Tell Thrilling Stories of Being Blown Into the Air Amid a Mass of Shattered Steel and Exploding Shells---Survivors Brought to Key West Scout the Idea of Accident---Spanish Officials Protest Too Much---Our Cabinet Orders a Searching Inquiry---Journal Sends Divers to Havana to Report Upon the Condition of the Wreck. Was the Vessel Anchored Over a Mine?

BY CAPTAIN E. L. ZALINSKI, U. S. A.

(Captain Zalinski is the inventor of the famous dynamite gun, which would be the principal factor in our coast defence in case of war.)

Assistant Secretary of the Navy Theodore Roosevelt says he is convinced that the destruction of the Maine in Havana Harbor was not an accident. The Journal offers a reward of $50,000 for exclusive evidence that will convict the person, persons or Government criminally responsible for the destruction of the American battle ship and the death of 258 of its crew.

The suspicion that the Maine was deliberately blown up grows stronger every hour. Not a single fact to the contrary has been produced.

Captain Sigsbee, of the Maine, and Consul-General Lee both urge that public opinion be suspended until they have completed their investigation. They are taking the course of tactful men who are convinced that there has been treachery.

Washington reports very late that Captain Sigsbee had feared some such event as a hidden mine. The English cipher code was used all day yesterday by the naval officers in cabling instead of the usual American code.

When the U.S. battleship Maine was sunk in Havana Harbor on February 15, 1898, American newspapers vied with each other in reporting the disaster.

As yet the cause of the explosion is not apparent.

The wounded sailors of the *Maine* are unable to explain it. It is believed that the cruiser is totally destroyed.

The explosion shook the whole city. The windows were broken in all the houses.

The correspondent of the Associated Press says he has conversed with several of the wounded sailors. He understands from them that the explosion took place while they were asleep, so that they can give no particulars as to the cause.

Captain C. D. Sigsbee, commander of the *Maine*, cabled Secretary Long:

Captain cables that some were killed and many wounded, and that the Spanish soldiers and sailors did everything in their power to rescue those who were thrown into the water. Moreover, the captain's dispatch speaks of the great kindness of the officials and citizens of Havana, who showered attention upon the sufferers. They cared tenderly for the wounded. The captain in his dispatch also tells of the heroic work of the officers and men of the cruiser Mongo.

Spain's Populace Hostile to the United States

The *Herald's* special correspondent at Madrid says a firm conviction prevails that this government will force a war. Bombardment of our coasts discussed— Spaniards counting upon the supposed helpless condition of all American towns except New York.

Special Cable to the Herald

Talk of bombarding our coasts. At the same time the ships of war could bombard the coast towns which, with the exception of New York, are considered unprotected, the United States not having sufficient warships to protect them. At the same time, also, great calculations are made on the widespread role which would fall upon the businessmen in the United States, whereas the bourse [stock exchange] here would scarcely change, as was the case with the United States. It would merely be the first step toward the solution of the question, which is slowly bleeding the resources of the country to death.

Such is the representative idea of the public Spanish feeling today but, mark you, do not quote it as the government's.

A MESSAGE FROM PRESIDENT WILLIAM MCKINLEY TO THE CONGRESS OF THE UNITED STATES[17]

On March 28, 1898, President William McKinley reported to a joint session of the U.S. Congress. A naval court of inquiry had been organized and a thorough investigation had been made into the *Maine* disaster. The court of inquiry had concluded that the ship was destroyed by a submarine mine. The president's speech was obviously a preliminary to a declaration of war by the United States against Spain.

For some time prior to the visit of the *Maine* to Havana harbor, our consular representatives pointed out the advantages to flow from the visit of national ships to the Cuban waters, in accustoming the people to the presence of our flag as a symbol of goodwill and of our ships in the fulfillment of the mission of protection to

The twisted wreckage of the Maine *remains afloat in Havana Harbor the day after the explosion.*

American interests, even though no immediate need therefor might exist.

Accordingly, on the 24th of January last, after a conference with the Spanish minister, in which the renewal of visits of our war vessels to Spanish waters was discussed and accepted, the peninsular authorities at Madrid and Havana were advised of the purpose of this government to resume friendly naval visits at Cuban ports, and in that view the *Maine* would forthwith call at the port of Havana. This announcement was received by the Spanish government with appreciation of the friendly character of the visit of the *Maine*, and with notification of intention to return the courtesy by sending Spanish ships to the principal ports of the United States. Meanwhile, the *Maine* entered the port of Havana on the 25th of January, her arrival being marked with no special incident besides the exchange of customary salutes and ceremonial visits.

The *Maine* continued in the harbor of Havana during the three weeks following her arrival, and no appreciable excitement attended her stay; on the contrary, a feeling of relief and confidence followed the resumption of the long-interrupted friendly intercourse. So noticeable was this immediate effect of her visit that the consul general strongly urged that the presence of our ships in Cuban waters should be kept up by retaining the *Maine* at Havana or, in the event of her recall, by sending another vessel there to take her place.

At forty minutes past nine on the evening of the 15th of February, the *Maine* was destroyed by an explosion, by which the entire forward part of the ship was utterly wrecked. In this catastrophe, two officers and two hundred and sixty-four of her crew perished, those who were not killed outright by her explosion being pinned between decks by the tangle of wreckage and drowned by the immediate sinking of the hull.

Prompt assistance was rendered by the neighboring vessels anchored in the harbor, aid being especially given by the boats of the Spanish cruiser *Alfonso XII*, and the Ward Line steamer *The City of Washington*, which lay not far distant. The wounded were generously cared for by the authorities of Havana, the hospitals being freely open to them, while the earliest recovered bodies of the dead were interred by the municipality in the public cemetery in the city. Tributes of grief and sympathy were offered from all official quarters of the island.

The appalling calamity fell upon the people of our country with crushing force, and for a brief time an intense excitement prevailed, which in a community less just and self-controlled than ours might have led to hasty acts of blind resentment. This spirit, however, soon gave way to the calmer processes of reason and to the resolve to investigate the facts and await material proof before forming a judgment as to the cause, the responsibility, and, if the facts warranted, the remedy. This course necessarily recommended itself from the outset to the Executive, for only in the light of dispassionately ascertained certainty could it determine the nature and measure of its full duty in the matter.

The usual procedure was followed, as in all cases of casualty or disaster to national vessels of any maritime state. A naval court of inquiry was at once organized, composed of officers well qualified by rank and practical experience to discharge the duty imposed upon them. Aided by a strong force of wreckers and divers, the court proceeded to make a thorough investigation on the spot, employing every available means for the impartial and exact determination of the explosion. Its operations have been conducted with the utmost deliberation and judgment, and while independently pursued, no source of information was neglected and the fullest opportunity was allowed for a simultaneous investigation by the Spanish authorities.

The finding of the court of inquiry was reached after twenty-three days of continuous labor, on the 21st of March, and having been approved on the 22nd by the Commander in Chief of the United States naval force of the North Atlantic station, was transmitted to the Executive.

It is herewith laid before the Congress, together with the voluminous testimony laid before the court. Its purport is in brief as follows:

When the *Maine* arrived at Havana, she was conducted by the regular government pilot to buoy number

5, to which she was moored in from five and one half to six fathoms of water. The state of discipline on board and the condition of her magazines, boilers, coal bunkers, and storage compartments are passed in review with conclusion that excellent order prevailed and that no indication of any cause for an internal explosion existed in any quarter.

At eight o'clock on the evening of February 15th, everything had been reported secure and all was quiet. At forty minutes past nine o'clock, the vessel was suddenly destroyed. There were two distinct explosions with a brief interval between them. The first lifted the forward part of the ship very perceptibly; the second, which was more open, prolonged, and of greater volume, is attributed by the court to the partial explosion of two or more of the forward magazines. . . .

The conclusions of the court are: that the loss of the *Maine* was not in any respect due to the fault of [or to] negligence on the part of any of the officers or members of her crew;

That the ship was destroyed by the explosion of a submarine mine, which caused the partial explosion of two or more of her magazines; and

That no evidence has been attainable fixing the responsibility for the destruction of the *Maine* upon any person or persons.

I have directed that the findings of the court of inquiry and the views of this government thereon be communicated to the government of Her Majesty the Queen Regent [of Spain], and I do not permit myself to doubt that the sense of justice of the Spanish nation will dictate a course of action suggested by honor and the friendly relations of the two governments.

It will be the duty of the Executive to advise the Congress of the result, and in the meantime deliberate consideration is invoked.

William McKinley
Executive Mansion, March 28, 1898

THE CHARGE OF SAN JUAN HILL
BY RICHARD HARDING DAVIS[18]

Theodore Roosevelt, then assistant secretary of the navy, was a leader of those Americans who demanded military action against Spain in the wake of the *Maine* disaster. President William McKinley would have preferred a more cautious policy, but on April 25, 1898, the U.S. Congress voted to declare war on Spain.

Roosevelt volunteered immediately for active service, enlisting in the army with the rank of lieutenant colonel. He was assigned to the First U.S. Cavalry, a popular regiment known as the Rough Riders. Leonard Wood was the commanding officer, but Roosevelt, with his dramatic personality and spectacular courage, although only the second-in-command, caught the public imagination.

On July 1, 1898, eight thousand American troops had been blocked in their advance by a heavily fortified enemy position atop San Juan Hill. The Spaniards were aided in their defense by a smokeless fire that effectively hid their guns from the Americans.

Pinned down by murderous gunfire, the American troops were suffering heavy casualties. Around midday, Roosevelt and his Rough Riders arrived on the scene to save the situation. In the account that follows, Richard Harding Davis, a famous war correspondent of his day, gives an eyewitness account of the courage and daring of both the men and their leader. As a result of this famous battle, Theodore Roosevelt became a national hero and the capture of San Juan Hill became one of the most famous battles in U.S. history.

The situation was desperate. Our troops could not retreat, as the trail for two miles behind them was wedged with men. They could not remain where they were, for they were being shot to pieces. There was only one thing they could do—go forward and take San Juan Hill by assault. It was as desperate as the situation itself. To charge earthworks held by men with modern rifles and using modern artillery . . . and to attack them in advance and not in the flanks are both impossible military propositions. But this campaign had not been conducted according to military rules, and a series of military blunders had brought seven thousand American soldiers into a chute of death from which there was no escape except by taking the enemy who held it by the throat and driving him out and beating him down. So the generals of divisions and brigadiers stepped back and relinquished their commands to the regimental officers and the enlisted men.

"We can do nothing more," they virtually said. "There is the enemy."

Colonel Roosevelt, on horseback, broke from the woods behind the lines of the Ninth and, finding its men lying in his way, shouted: "If you don't want to go forward, let my men pass, please." The junior officers of the Ninth, with their Negroes, instantly sprang into line with the Rough Riders and charged at the blockhouse on the right.

Roosevelt, mounted high on horseback and charging the rifle pits at a gallop and quite alone, made you feel that you would like to cheer. He wore on his sombrero a blue polka-dot handkerchief which, as he advanced, floated out straight behind his head, like a guidon. Afterward the men of his regiment, who [had] followed his flag, adopted a polka-dot handkerchief as the badge of the Rough Riders. Someone asked one of the officers if he had any difficulty in making his men follow him. "No," he answered. "I had some difficulty in keeping up with them." As one of the brigade generals said: "San Juan was won by regimental officers and men. We had as little to do as the referee at a prize-fight who calls 'time!' We called 'time,' and they did the fighting."

I have seen many illustrations and pictures of the charge on the San Juan hills, but none of them seem to show it just as I remembered it. In the picture papers, the men are running uphill swiftly and gallantly, in regular formation, rank after rank, with flags flying, their eyes aflame, and their hair streaming, their bayonets fixed, in long brilliant lines and [with the] invincible, overpowering weight of numbers. Instead of which I think the thing which impressed one the most, when our men started from cover, was that they were so few. It seemed as if someone had made an awful and terrible mistake. One's instinct was to call to them to come back. You felt that someone had blundered and that these few men were blindly following out some madman's mad order. It was not heroic then; it seemed merely terribly pathetic. The pity of it, the folly of such a sacrifice, was what held you.

They had no glittering bayonets, they were not massed in regular array. There were a few men in advance, bunched together and creeping up a steep, sunny hill, the top of which roared and flashed with flame. The men held their guns across their breasts and stepped heavily as they climbed. Behind these first few, spreading out like a fan, were single lines of men, slipping and scrambling in the smooth grass, moving forward with difficulty, as though they were walking waist high through water, moving slowly, carefully, with strenuous effort. It was much more wonderful than any swinging charge could have been. They walked to greet death at every step, many of them, as they advanced, sinking suddenly or pitching forward and disappearing in the high grass, but the others waded on, stubbornly forming a thin blue line that kept creeping higher and higher up the hill. It was as inevitable as the rising tide. It was a miracle of self-sacrifice, a triumph of bulldog courage, which one watched breathless with wonder. The fire of the Spanish riflemen, who still stuck bravely to their posts, doubled and trebled in fierceness, the crests of the hills crackled and burst in amazed roars and rippled with waves of tiny flames. But the blue lines crept steadily on and on, and then, near the top, the broken fragments gathered together with a sudden burst of speed, the Spaniards appeared for a moment outlined against the sky and, posed for instant flight, fired a last volley and fled before the swift-moving wave that leaped and sprang after them.

The men of the Ninth and the Rough Riders rushed to the blockhouse together, the men of the Sixth, of the Third, of the Tenth Cavalry, of the Sixth and Sixteenth Infantry, fell on their faces along the crest of the hills beyond and opened fire upon the vanishing enemy. They drove the yellow silk flag of the cavalry and the Stars and Stripes of their country into the soft earth of the trenches and then sank down and looked back at the road they had climbed and swung their hats in the air. And from far overhead, from those few figures perched on the Spanish rifle pits, with their flags planted among the empty cartridges of the enemy, and overlooking the walls of Santiago, came faintly, the sound of a tired, broken cheer.

Song of the American Soldier in Cuba

Trooper Guy Scull of Boston would bring out his banjo and then through the dust and the mosquitoes rose an old Harvard tune with new words.

Oh, those good old days of eighteen ninety-eight
When we fit for Colonel Wood by gosh!
When we fit for Colonel Wood.
Those good old days when we fit for Colonel Wood.

How well we remember the year ninety-eight

When the cowboys rode out of the West
The Spanish sent a cannonball a-whizzing through
    the air
That struck Roosevelt through the heart.
Then up jumped Teddy. Says he: "I am not dead!
I'm sure they could not kill me if they would."

Oh, those good old days of ninety-eight
When we fit for Colonel Wood,
When we fit for Colonel Wood.
Those good old days of eighteen ninety-eight
When we fit for Colonel Wood.

HOW CUBA WON
SELF-DETERMINATION
BY LEONARD WOOD[19]

In 1899, General Leonard Wood, just recently promoted from colonel to general, was appointed representative of the American military occupation in Cuba in Oriente province. Conditions at the time of his takeover were catastrophic. Diseases of all kinds were rampant, thousands of people were dying, there was practically no food available for the population, and there was no work for those able and willing to work. Schools were not functioning, and the administration of justice had come to a halt. Wood, who was a doctor as well as a general, was a man of outstanding ability and seemingly unlimited energy. Taking charge, he arranged for the sick to be cared for, for the hungry to be fed, for courts to reopen, and for schools to function. For those who wanted to work, it became possible to find work. After only a year the terrible

I

The purpose of our military government of Cuba, after the Spanish War, was to prepare the Cubans for self-government and to establish conditions which would render the establishment of a Cuban republic possible and its orderly and successful maintenance probable. The occupation of Cuba began with the occupation of the city of Santiago and extended rapidly over the province of the same name [now called Oriente Province]. The territory occupied by the military forces of the United States prior to the general transfer of the island, January 1, 1899, was limited to this province. Conditions in Santiago at the time of occupancy were as unfavorable as can be imagined. Yellow fever, pernicious malaria, and intestinal fevers were all prevalent to an alarming extent. The city and surrounding country were full of sick Spanish soldiers, starving Cubans, and the sick of their own army. The sanitary conditions were indescribably bad. There was little or no water available, and the conditions were such as can be imagined to exist in a tropical city following a siege and capture in the most unhealthy season of the year.

The first work undertaken was feeding the starving, taking care of the sick, cleaning up and removing the dangerous material in the city. In addition to correcting these local conditions, it was necessary to send food and medicine throughout the province, maintain order, reestablish municipal government, reorganize the courts, and do the thousand and one things incident to reestablishing the semblance of government in a stricken and demoralized community. The actual difficulties were increased by the fact that the people with whom we had to deal spoke a foreign language with which few of us were familiar. The death rate among our own troops was heavy and the percentage of sick appalling. The regulars and volunteers engaged in the siege and capture of the city were withdrawn late in August and their places filled with one regiment of regulars and a number of regiments of volunteers. The arrival of these green troops in the height of the unhealthy season was a cause of grave anxiety and their care required unusual precautions. By this time, the city had been cleaned [and] the death rate greatly checked; food had been sent by pack train to the interior and by sea to the various seaport towns of the province, and couriers had been sent through the country to inform the inhabitants where they could procure food and medicine; custom houses had been established at all the ports, and with the funds collected from this source, public works had already been undertaken.

II

The first public works were carried out in the city of Santiago to drain unhealthy surroundings of the city, improve the water supply, and render the place more habitable. The purpose of the public works was not only to improve conditions but to give occupation to the thousands of idle people, including disbanded soldiers of the Cuban army. Some were paid in money and some in rations. Every effort was made to get the people out to their homes in the country, and with this in view, men were furnished with a few agricultural implements and food enough for a month and sent out to their homes. In this way, thousands of idle people about the city were disposed of and placed upon their own property, and surrounded with those members of their families who had survived the war and its consequences.

A rural guard composed of Cubans was rapidly organized for the maintenance of order in the rural districts. During this period, troops were also used for this purpose. As soon as conditions of actual starvation had been done away with and the worst features of the sanitary situation improved, steps were taken to organize municipal government in the various towns. There was no time to write an electoral law and put it in force. The method adopted was to go to a town, assemble from sixty to one hundred men representing all classes of the people, and ask them to name municipal officers and to present their list as soon as completed. In this way, the officials of all the municipalities of the province were in time appointed. Temporary regulations were drawn up governing local taxation. Stores and business houses were divided into classes and were required to pay so much a month to the municipal treasury. Under the means so procured, municipal governments were started. Expenses were kept at the lowest figure.

III

As soon as a municipal government was organized, steps were taken to temporarily relieve the situation in each municipality, and medicine, food, and assistance were given those most needful of it. The next step was to establish village schools in all the different towns.

IV

At the end of the year the province was orderly and fairly healthy, municipal governments were running, with rather crude machinery to be sure, but performing the necessary functions. Nearly two hundred public schools had been established, and all incurred expenses had been paid from revenues collected, and approximately $60,000 was on hand for carrying out certain sanitary work in the city of Santiago, for which arrangements had been made. The Supreme Court, court of first instance for municipal courts, had been established throughout the province. Custom houses were in operation, and starvation had disappeared. A proclamation embodying the general principles of a Bill of Rights had been published, giving the people the right to carry arms, to hold public meetings, and in fact, to do all things which people do under free governments. Such was the condition in the province of Santiago at the time of the transfer of the island to the United States on January 1, 1899.

V

The government was transferred eventually to the Cuban people exactly as promised, with no debt but, of course, some current liabilities for public works in process of construction, and with $1,613,000 free for allotment. Approximately 97 percent of the officials were Cuban, and they proved loyal and efficient and honest. The courts of justice were entirely in the hands of the people. The attitude of the Spanish element was always friendly. They represent the bulk of the business interests of the island. They are people of order, and make excellent citizens.

VI

The government was transferred as a going concern. All the public offices were filled with competent, well-trained employees; the island was free from debt, had a surplus of a million and a half dollars in the treasury, and was possessed of thoroughly trained and efficient personnel in all departments; completely equipped buildings [were available] for the transaction of public business, the administration of justice was free, habeas corpus had been put in force, and police courts had been established; a new marriage law on lines proposed by the Roman Catholic bishop of Havana, giving equal rights to all denominations, was in operation; the people were governed, in all municipalities, by officials of their own choice elected at the polls; trials in Cuban courts were as prompt as in any state of the Union, and life and property were absolutely safe; sanitary conditions were better than those existing in most parts of the United States; yellow fever had been eradicated from the island; modern systems of public education, including a university, high schools, and nearly 3,700 public schools had been established; [there were] also well-organized departments of charity and public works. The island was well supplied with hospitals and asylums, and beggars were almost unknown. A new railway law had been promulgated; custom houses had been equipped and thoroughly established; the great question of church property had been settled; a basis of agreement between mortgaged creditors and debtors had been established; municipalities had been reduced from 138 to 82 in number; public order was excellent; the island possessed a highly organized and efficient rural guard; an enormous amount of public works had been undertaken and completed; harbors and channels were buoyed; old lighthouses had been thoroughly renovated and new ones built; in short, the government as transferred was in excellent running order. The great expense of organization and equipment was borne by the military government. At the time of the transfer, government buildings and equipment of every description were in such condition as to be able to render useful services for years at a small outlay compared to the cost incurred by the military government in renovating, building, and purchasing the same. The insular government was undertaken without a dollar of public money on hand, except the daily collections of customs and internal revenue, and involved the collection and disbursement of $57,107,140.80, during its existence, for improvements in material conditions and the upbuilding of insular institutions. This sum does not include the municipal revenues, only the general insular revenues.

VII

The work called for and accomplished was the building of a republic in a country where approximately 70 percent of the people were illiterate; where they had lived always as a military colony; where general elections, as we understand them, were unknown; in fact, it was a work which called for practically a rewriting of the administrative law of the land, including the law of charities and hospitals, public works, sanitary law, school law, railway law, etc.; meeting and controlling the worst possible sanitary conditions; putting the people to school; writing an electoral law and training the people in the use of it; establishing an entirely new system of accounting and auditing; the election and assembling of representatives of the people to draw up and adopt a constitution for the proposed new republic; in short, the establishment, in a little over three years, in a Latin military colony, in one of the most unhealthy countries of the world, of a republic modeled closely upon the lines of our own great Anglo-Saxon republic; and the transfer to the Cuban people of the republic so established, free from debt, healthy, orderly, well equipped, and with a good balance in the treasury. All of this work was accomplished without serious friction. The island of Cuba was transferred to its people as promised and was started on its career in good condition and under the most favorable circumstances.

The government of Cuba, while called "military,"

was so in name only. The courts excised full and untrammeled jurisdiction from first to last. Means of appeal to the Supreme Court of Cuba from the decisions of the military governor were provided in all cases except for appeals against such acts of the military government as were of a legislative character, such as the promulgation of laws, etc. Nearly all public offices were filled by Cubans, and the government, as conducted, was as nearly a government by the people as was possible under existing conditions.

REPORT OF THE DEPARTMENT OF SANITATION: YELLOW FEVER BY MAJOR W. C. GORGAS, MEDICAL CORPS U.S.A.[20]

One of the great successes achieved by the U.S. military government in Cuba under Leonard Wood was the almost complete eradication of yellow fever. Even before the time of Columbus, this terrible disease had killed thousands of Cubans each year. Cargo ships coming from Havana had also exported yellow fever to many cities in the United States. In 1793, for instance, an epidemic of yellow fever broke out in Philadelphia, killing one-tenth of its citizens. No one knew what caused this lethal illness; no one knew how it could be treated.

In 1900 a fresh epidemic of yellow fever swept Cuba. General Wood, the leader of the American intervention, was also a doctor. Determined to discover what caused the illness and so learn how to treat it, General Wood asked Dr. Walter Reed and a team of army surgeons to study the latest outbreak.

Dr. Carlos Finlay, a Cuban doctor, believed the disease was carried from person to person by the sting of a certain type of mosquito. Convinced by Finlay's arguments, Dr. Reed decided to try out his theory. A series of experiments were done under Dr. Reed's direction, and some brave men volunteered to undergo them. In the course of these tests, one man died, but beyond any doubt, Dr. Finlay's theory was proved correct.

If the Americans had accomplished nothing else in Cuba, this discovery, which saved thousands of lives each year, would have made the intervention a success. For the first time it was possible to prevent yellow fever. The illness was conquered not only in Cuba but wherever there was an outbreak throughout the world.

All the tables of this report show a steady and general improvement in the sanitary condition of the city, but the great work done this year by the Department has been the extirpation of yellow fever from Havana, and this has been due to measures for the first time adopted and carried out here, based upon certain scientific facts established by the army board of which Major Walter Reed was president. If we are right in our belief that, by measures taken for the killing of infected mosquitoes, we have rid Havana of yellow fever in a few months, when it had been endemic in the city for the past two hundred years, it is of vast importance that these facts should be made known to the world as rapidly as possible, and this is particularly true with regard to the United States. For it may happen that during the coming summer, yellow fever might be introduced into our southern cities, and if it can be controlled, as it has been in Havana during the past year, it would save many lives and prevent financial loss to the states so affected.

To make clear our claim that Havana has been purged of yellow fever during the past year by the destruction of infected mosquitoes, I will run over in brief, the history of Havana with regard to yellow fever during the past one hundred years and point out that yellow fever has always been endemic in Havana up to 1901; that sanitary measures, which had reduced the excessive death rate of Havana to that of healthy cities of civilized countries, had had little or no effect upon yellow fever; that general disinfection, as carried out for other infections and contagious diseases, had been extensively and faithfully tried, that yellow fever had suddenly and sharply disappeared, upon the introduction of a system whose object was killing infected mosquitoes, based upon the theory that the stegomyia mosquito is the *only* means of transmitting yellow fever; that from September 28 to February 15, the time of making this report, there has not been a single case of yellow fever in Havana, a condition of affairs so unusual that all question of chance can be dropped from consideration.

The winter epidemic in 1899 was unusually severe. The next year, 1900, there were 310 deaths from yellow fever. This demonstrates that the general sanitary measures taken had a marked effect upon the general death rate, but very little upon the death rate for yellow fever.

At the beginning of 1901, the prospects, as far as yellow fever was concerned, were very unfavorable. There was a large nonimmune population, probably larger than it had ever been before. The city was thoroughly infected, cases having occurred in all parts. During the preceding year, there had been 1,244 cases and 310 deaths.

January commenced with an unusually large number of deaths from this disease; February was equally severe. The military governor, being determined that no precaution should be omitted, directed that, in addition to former [sanitary] measures, work be started on the line that the mosquito was the cause of transmission of the disease. This work went into effect about the first of March, with the result that during the whole year we had only eighteen deaths from yellow fever, and twelve of these eighteen deaths occurred before the mosquito measures were started.

This is still better shown by taking the table of deaths, which estimates the yellow fever year as commencing in April 1. In this we see that for the past eleven years, the maximum 1,385 deaths occurred in 1896–1897; the minimum 122 deaths in 1899–1900. For the year 1901–1902, up to February 15, there were five deaths. This difference is too marked to be any matter of chance. That the yellow fever of 1901–1902 had only 1/25 of the number of deaths that had occurred in the minimum year of the preceding eleven years must be due to some cause that did not act during these years. Still more marked is the fact that since September 28, 1901, no cases at all have occurred, particularly when it is considered that October and November rank among the worst months for yellow fever.

THE GOOD NEIGHBOR POLICY
BY SUMNER WELLES[21]

In August 1933, Cuba was once again in turmoil. Concerned with the deepening crisis that threatened to erupt into out-

In November 1933, Sumner Welles (left), U.S. Ambassador to Cuba, and President Franklin Roosevelt take a ride after discussing the potentially volatile general strike then occurring in Cuba. Discontent was rampant in Cuba at the time.

right civil war, President Franklin Roosevelt appointed his assistant secretary of state, Sumner Welles, to serve as ambassador to Cuba.

Due to widespread graft and discontent, the Machado government fell. Martial law was declared. There was no food, all shops were closed, no trains ran, there was no post or telegraph. A general strike was called.

The strike resolved itself into a nationwide protest against the corruption of the Machado government. Havana was like a besieged city.

Sumner Welles was in constant communication with President Roosevelt, who was working to avoid intervention. He urged Cuban president Gerardo Machado to ask for a leave of absence. Machado refused. On August 10, President Roosevelt threatened to send troops into Cuba within twenty-four hours.

In order to avoid bloodshed, the Cuban army deposed President Machado and demanded that he resign. A few hours later he handed in his resignation.

Hundreds of citizens gathered in front of the American embassy to show their appreciation for the help the United States had given. Sumner Welles, in the name of the American government, promised to continue mediation and urged control and calm.

In the account that follows, Ambassador Welles reports on the chaotic conditions he found upon his arrival in Cuba. The island was in a state of virtual anarchy. Throughout the crisis, Roosevelt consulted with all the other American republics, an important decision that became known as the Good Neighbor Policy.

I was appointed United States ambassador to Cuba in April of 1933. I remember the final conversation I had with the president [Franklin Roosevelt] in his study in the White House the night before my departure. His sympathy for the Cuban people was deep and real. He hoped that the government and the leaders of the opposition parties and groups might be persuaded to reach an agreement upon a course of procedure which would make it possible, through the methods afforded by the Constitution, for a change of administration to take place. This would give the people of Cuba the opportunity to start afresh under new auspices.

It is impossible here to touch briefly upon the salient events of that dramatic summer of 1933 in Cuba. President Gerardo Machado was undoubtedly a type that would have been of interest to any psychiatrist. He was a man of vigor and of force, utterly autocratic and reactionary in his beliefs, and motivated, I think, primarily by a feeling of burning resentment that the early popularity which he had enjoyed should have turned into violent popular hatred. His life was in constant danger. His movement from the palace in Havana to his country place in the outskirts of the capital had to be surreptitious. In the frequent conversations I had with him, in which time and time again there came up for discussion the revolting details of the murders committed by his secret police, particularly those of young patriots hardly more than boys, he never gave the slightest indication that these acts of barbaric cruelty were anything but justified. In the last days of his tenure of office, a shocking incident occurred. The police of Havana fired upon a completely unarmed and orderly crowd marching in demonstration on one of the main avenues of Havana, killing many innocent persons. I remember particularly how Machado brushed aside the incident as of no importance. He added: "As a matter of fact, more than half of those killed were not even Cubans; [they] were foreigners."

In the early days of August a spontaneous mutiny of the Cuban army took the matter out of his hands and he was forced to flee from Cuba on August 12. Mob rule prevailed in Havana and in many other regions for several days before order could once more be restored.

In the meantime, however, by the free designation of the heads of the opposition parties, Dr. Carlos Manuel de Céspedes became provisional president.

During the brief anarchic period through which Cuba passed in August of 1933, there were, of course, innumerable demands for American armed intervention; every request was rejected flatly. As a precautionary measure, however, President Roosevelt directed that certain vessels of the U.S. Navy be sent to Cuban waters to take away any American citizens or other foreigners whose lives might be endangered. At the time, the president created the precedent for what was to become the studied policy of his administration—consultation with the other American republics whenever the United States should find itself in a position where it might be obliged to take action affecting any other people of the Americas. The president summoned to the White House all the diplomatic representatives of the other American republics then in Washington and informed them frankly and in the fullest detail of the situation which had arisen in Cuba. He told them that, while the United States would not avail itself of its treaty right to intervene [as agreed upon in the Platt Amendment], a situation threatened to develop which might give rise to a breakdown of orderly government.

At the beginning of September, however, the constructive efforts of the Céspedes government to relieve the appalling distress of the Cuban people were suddenly arrested by a second mutiny in the Cuban army. This time it was a mutiny led by noncommissioned officers against the commissioned officers, the great majority of whom were regarded as having been directly responsible for the excesses of the Machado government. The second mutiny was led, and to a very considerable extent planned, by that extraordinarily brilliant and able figure, Fulgencio Batista. [Batista was elected president of Cuba in 1940.]

HISTORY WILL ABSOLVE ME
BY FIDEL CASTRO[22]

In the early morning of July 26, 1953, Fidel Castro, at the head of a band of 125 student idealists, attempted to launch a coup against the corrupt Batista regime. The plan was to take over the City Hospital, the Palace of Justice, and the Moncada Barracks.

The plan failed. Castro's men, outnumbered fifteen to one, were defeated. Many were taken prisoner, tortured, and executed. Fidel Castro, his brother Raúl, and others were arrested.

On October 16, 1953, Fidel Castro was tried alone in a small room in the Santiago City Hospital before three judges, two public prosecutors, and six journalists. In his own defense Castro delivered a passionate and eloquent speech that lasted five hours. It did not change the verdict, however, which had been decided in advance. Castro was sentenced to fifteen years at the notorious Isle of Pines prison.

Later, after being granted amnesty, Castro sought refuge in Mexico, where he assembled a small band of Cuban patriots. In December 1956, just thirty-eight months after his trial, Castro and a band of eighty-two Cuban patriots landed in Oriente Province, ready once again to risk their lives in an attempt to unseat the dictator Batista.

The excerpt that follows is taken from Castro's defense speech before his accusers in that small room at the Santiago City Hospital.

Twenty-two Cuban exiles arrested for plotting the assassination of President Fulgencio Batista were photographed in June 1956. The arrow points to Fidel Castro, a young revolutionary at the time.

As soon as Santiago de Cuba was in our hands, we would immediately have readied the people for war. Bayamo was attacked precisely to locate our advance forces along the Cauto River.

The people we counted on in our struggle were these:

Seven hundred thousand Cubans without work,

who desire to earn their daily bread honestly without having to emigrate in search of a livelihood.

Five hundred thousand farm laborers inhabiting miserable shacks, who work four months of the year and starve during the rest, sharing their misery with their children who have not an inch of land to till and whose existence would move any heart not made of stone.

Four hundred thousand industrial laborers and stevedores whose retirement funds have been embezzled, whose benefits are being taken away, whose homes are wretched quarters, whose salaries pass from the hands of the boss to those of the moneylender, whose future is a pay reduction and dismissal, whose life is eternal work, and whose only rest is in the tomb.

One hundred thousand small farmers who live and die working on land that is not theirs, looking at it with sadness as Moses looked at the promised land, to die without ever owning it; who, like feudal serfs, have to pay for the use of their parcel of land by giving up a portion of its products; who cannot love it, improve it, beautify it, nor plant a lemon or an orange tree on it because they never know when a sheriff will come with the rural guard to evict them from it.

Thirty thousand teachers and professors who are so devoted, dedicated, and necessary to the better destiny of future generations and who are so badly treated and paid.

Twenty thousand small businessmen, weighted down by debts, ruined by the crisis, and harangued by a plague of grafting and venal officials.

Ten thousand young professionals, doctors, engineers, lawyers, veterinarians, teachers, dentists, pharmacists, newspaper men, painters, [and] sculptors who come forth from school with their degree, anxious to work and full of hope, only to find themselves at a dead end with all doors closed and where no ear hears their clamor or supplication.

These are the people, the ones who know misfortune and therefore are capable of fighting with limitless courage. . . .

The Declaration of Independence of the Congress of Philadelphia on July Fourth 1776, consecrated this right [to rebel] in a beautiful paragraph which reads: "We hold these truths to be self-evident, that all men are created equal, that they are endowed by their Creator with certain unalienable Rights, that among these are Life, Liberty and the pursuit of Happiness. —That to secure these rights, Governments are instituted among Men, deriving their just powers from the consent of the governed,—That whenever any Form of Government becomes destructive of these ends, it is the Right of the People to alter or to abolish it and to institute new Government, laying its foundation on such principles and organizing its powers in such form as to them shall seem most likely to effect their Safety and Happiness."

The famous French Declaration of the Rights of Man will send this principle to the coming generations: "When the Government violates the rights of the people, insurrection is for them the most sacred of rights and the most imperative of duties. When a person seizes sovereignty, he should be condemned to death by free men."

I know that imprisonment will be as hard for me as it has ever been for anyone, filled with cowardly threats and wicked torture. But I do not fear prison, as I do not fear the fury of the miserable tyrant [Fulgencio Batista, president of Cuba] who took the lives of seventy of my comrades.

Condemn me. It does not matter. History will absolve me.

STUDENT REVOLUTIONARIES BATTLE THE POLICE BY JOSE LUIS LLOVIO-MENENDEZ[23]

José Luis Llovio-Menendez was a medical student at Havana University during the oppressive and brutal dictatorship of Fulgencio Batista (1939–59). Like many of his fellow students he was an ardent revolutionary. In the excerpt that follows, written in 1955, he describes one of the valiant if reckless demonstrations that the unarmed students staged against Batista's well-armed police.

Under Batista, as I saw for myself . . . the rich thrived and the poor remained forgotten. Corruption spread uncontrollably while repression, crime, and cruelty became the weapons of the dictator's authority.

These problems, which we students discussed endlessly, united us in our common desire to eradicate them, to build a better Cuba. We believed in radical change through a democratic revolution that would forever end the gross poverty, corruption, official violence, authoritarianism, and foreign interference we saw every day. In a country with more than enough natural resources to provide for all its citizens, it seemed only just that there be equal opportunity for everyone. This wasn't an academic position on our part. We fervently believed in this ideal and were ready to give our lives for it.

In the early months of the dictatorship, the sharpest expressions of the student rebellion were demonstrated in Havana. Beginning for me with the manifestation of November 27, 1953, these marches were nearly constant and always exuberantly reckless. We would gather on campus at the Plaza Cárdenas behind the rectory. Then, at the appointed moment, the students would form themselves into rows and, with linked arms, march from Alma Mater down the great steps to San Lazaro Street.

All the way we'd sing the Cuban national anthem, often to the enthusiastic encouragement of the neighborhood's residents, who cheered us from their balconies. Sometimes student snipers were stationed above them on the roof to open fire if the police dared violate the campus's autonomy.

Usually the police would be waiting for us three blocks from the steps, at the edge of the university, where they would reroute traffic and line up their patrol cars. After we had finished singing the anthem, we would bear down on them shouting antigovernment slogans. Once we were outside the university property, they waded into us with their clubs and fists, firing their weapons into the air and training enormous fire hoses on us. In the end they usually succeeded in dispersing the students, sending us running down adjacent streets looking for protection from a sympathetic neighbor.

Those were the days of relative restraint by Batista's police. But in 1955 an inexorable spiral of violence began in earnest.

I recall a typical incident from December of that year. Several of us who had been carrying that day's banner were cut off by the police. I ran down a street with several officers in chase, threatening to shoot me if I didn't stop. At Infanta Street, I leapt for the window of a passing bus and shouted to the driver to stop and let me in.

Most of the drivers could still be counted on for such help—this bus stopped for me—but in the growing repression they soon chose to ignore fleeing students lest they suffer themselves if the police identified them as helping us.

Three blocks on, I saw several of the policemen savagely kicking and beating the vaguely human shape of a demented old beggar, familiar to everyone in the area. In his troubled wanderings through this part of Vevado, the old man would periodically shout: "Batista! The son of a bitch!"

Enraged at what I saw, I jumped from the bus, ran to the beggar, and then punched one of the policemen in the face, knocking him back several feet into a fried-food stand on the corner. Amid the sound of shattering glass and cries from the police and the food-stand owner, I knelt to help the old man to his feet. Suddenly I felt a shooting pain in my head.

Some hours later I awoke in the student clinic at the Calixto García Hospital nearby. As my senses cleared, I discovered that I had three broken ribs and that my face was bruised and badly swollen. According to those who'd witnessed the incident, my head injuries came from a policeman's club, and the broken ribs were a further courtesy from the officer and his friends, who had kicked me until they were tired of the sport.

Several of us from the manifestation had been taken to the clinic that day. I recognized one boy from past demonstrations who seemed to be in good humor despite the bullet in his leg.

"Listen," said Camillo in a jaunty voice, "what's happened to you? You look like Frankenstein." This was my introduction to the high-spirited Camillo Cienfuegos, a fellow revolutionary with whom I discussed politics passionately as we recovered from our injuries.

Camillo would soon leave Havana and reappear in the mountains with Fidel's small band. By 1958 he would rise to become the undisputed second-in-command of the Cuban Revolution.

A SWIM FOR CUBA
BY WARREN HINCKLE
AND WILLIAM TURNER[24]

In 1956 Fidel Castro was living in Mexico and trying to raise funds for his return to Cuba with an invasion force in the hope of overturning the corrupt and tyrannical government of Fulgencio Batista. To meet with ex-president Carlos Prío Socarrás, a multimillionaire and fellow exile who was based in McAllen, Texas, Castro had to swim the Rio Grande. Castro's mission was successful and he was able to fund his expedition.

The excerpt that follows—by Warren Hinckle, a former editor of *Ramparts* magazine, and William Turner, a former FBI agent—describes the meeting between the two exiles. The title of their book, *The Fish Is Red,* is taken from E. Howard Hunt's code phrase for the Bay of Pigs invasion, which took place several years after the meeting between Castro and Prío Socarrás.

In the noon hour heat of a September day in 1956, a tall man, wearing the clothes of a Mexican laborer, got out of a jalopy and stumbled down the incline to the river's edge. He stripped off his clothes and dashed into the dirty tan water [of the Rio Grande] with the vigor of a vacationer taking to the cool blue waves of the Riviera.

He swam frogman style with the strong, certain strokes of an accomplished swimmer. Behind him was the dusty Mexican border town of Reynosa; ahead, through the haze toward the United States side of the river, was the town of McAllen. As he approached the northern bank of the river, the swimmer submerged. For minutes there was no sign of him.

He surfaced in the midst of a motley crew of bathers, oil workers who had not bothered to remove their dungarees, splashing in the muddy water. The men surrounded the naked submariner and clasped him around the shoulders. Hand after callused hand joyously slapped his dripping back as he waded toward shore. A fresh set of clothes had been secreted away for him. The swim had been carefully arranged. The oil workers' bathing party was camouflage. The name of the mysterious wetback was Fidel Castro.

The man who walked into the lobby of the Hotel Casa de Palmas in McAllen could hardly have been the wretched creature who had climbed out of the river scarcely an hour before. The automobile ride into town had effected a transformation. The wetback had become a bourgeois gentleman of leisure returning from a round of golf at the country club; from the half smile set in his thick red lips, and the jaunty angle of his cigar protruding from them, it looked as though he had broken par. To the careful student of human anatomy, the victorious golfer bore a certain resemblance to the soaking-wet illegal alien; the athlete's poise . . . the long nose, coming straight down from his high forehead like a ski jump; the hypnotic brown eyes and scraggly chestnut hair, which, when excited, he shook the way a spirited horse tosses its head. He was clean-shaven except for a thin mustache that looked somehow out of place on so large a face still firm with the unlined flush of youth. A man would have guessed his age at about thirty. He was tall, very tall, and seemed higher than his six feet three inches. The illusion of size was generated by a magnetism that commanded attention and at the same time respect.

[Castro was admitted to Carlos Prío Socarrás's suite. The ex-president was a millionaire many times over. Both of them were in trouble with the Cuban authorities. The two men talked for hours.]

Castro was impatient. He paced up and down the room. He announced that he and his men were ready to attack Batista. All they needed was money. He talked at full speed, all energy and enthusiasm and concentration. When he finished, it was dark and Prío had agreed to give him $100,000.

Castro could hardly conceal his excitement. With the money he could buy new arms, he could bribe the Mexicans to leave him alone while he readied his invasion force, and he could buy a boat to float his revolution.

Castro got up to go. His comrades were waiting to sneak him back across the border into Mexico. Prío stopped him at the door. There was one last thing: there must be a united front against Batista. Prío volunteered to be in charge. He used all his considerable charm to put a bridle on the headstrong revolutionary. He extracted from Castro a promise to notify him when he was leaving for Cuba. "We will coordinate our activities," said Prío.

Castro nodded. He had no intention of letting this master of the spoils system look over his shoulder.

Prío also had his secrets. He did not tell Castro that he was organizing an invasion of Cuba from the Dominican Republic in league with the tyrant Trujillo; he would align himself with the very devil to get back into power. His hope was to beat his new ally to the revolutionary punch. Prío was businesslike about everything, none the less about revolutions; the money given to Castro, was, to him, a $100,000 insurance policy.

The two Cubans parted smiling, with faint lies on their lips.

THE GRANMA SAILS
TO LIBERATE CUBA
BY TAD SZULC[25]

At 1:30 A.M. on November 25, 1956, Fidel Castro and a small band of followers boarded their white yacht, the *Granma*, left their Mexican base, and sailed toward the open sea. Their mission was to liberate Cuba from the dictatorial rule of Fulgencio Batista.

It was a stormy night, and the *Granma's* crossing from the Mexican coast to Oriente Province was a near disaster. The weather was foul, and a ship that was built to carry twenty-five passengers was transporting eighty-two men together with their arms and supplies. Overloaded and undermanned, the yacht took seven days and four hours to reach its destination instead of the five days and nights that Fidel Castro had planned.

Tad Szulc was a reporter for Latin America for *The New York Times*.

For the expeditionaries, the horror began the instant they entered the Gulf of Mexico, just before daybreak on November 25. They hailed the open water by singing the Cuban national anthem and the 26th of July, marching and shouting, *"Viva la Revolucion!"* and "Down with the Batista dictatorship!" Then the sea attacked them. Immediately, most of the men became violently seasick. . . . They were not a fighting force, just a band of very sick men.

Che Guevara wrote that "the entire boat has a ridiculously tragic aspect: men with anguish reflected in their faces, grabbing their stomachs; some with their heads inside buckets, and other fallen in the strangest positions, motionless, their clothes filthy from vomit . . . except for the two or three sailors and four or five others, the rest of the contingent were seasick." Che, Fidel, and Faustino Perez were among those who did not succumb to illness; Guevara frantically searched the ship for antihistamines for the men, but there were none. Then the *Granma* began to take on water, the pump turned out to be broken, and they had to bail water with two buckets until the leak was located and fixed. On the third day the weather improved, and Castro ordered rifles calibrated again and some firing exercises began.

At dawn on Friday, November 30, the expedition was cruising toward Grand Cayman Island, only three-fourths of the way to the landing zone. Niquero and Pilon, 26th of July Movement members, awaited Castro in vain that dawn on the beaches in Cuba.

Late at night on Saturday, December 1, the white yacht was wallowing in high seas as she approached the Oriente coast in darkness: no moon and no visible coastal lights. Castro ordered the rebels to change into their olive green uniforms and he distributed the weapons. Crewmen kept climbing to the roof of the cabin to spot the Cabo Cruz lighthouse for a navigational fix—Cabo Cruz is on the southwestern tip of the Oriente Coast—when Roberto Roque, the navigator, slipped and fell overboard. Castro ordered the *Granma* to undertake a search for Roque despite the darkness. After sailing in circles for an hour, the rebels heard a weak voice respond to their calls, and incredibly they found him, using only a lantern shining over the waves. Che Guevara and Faustino Perez, both physicians, revived the nearly drowned Roque, and Castro proclaimed that now they were on to victory.

Resuming its careful progress toward the coast,

Granma entered the Niquero channel, but as he noted the buoys, Captain Pino realized that his charts were wrong, and he did not know the way. The dawn of Sunday, December 2, was just breaking when the yacht suddenly hit mud at low tide and came to a dead halt at 4:20 A.M. The spot was Los Cayuelos, more than a mile south of the beach where Castro had wanted to land (and just below the ironically named Purgatorio Point). The men were ordered to jump into the water, carrying only their personal weapons. All the heavy equipment and stores were left behind. René Rodriguez, slight of build was the first to go, and the bottom held him; the much heavier Castro followed, sinking up to his hips in the mud. Che Guevara remarked later, "This wasn't a landing, it was a shipwreck." The yacht was stuck some hundred yards from what appeared to be the coast, and Fidel and his men managed to wade to it. Che Guevara and Raúl Castro were the last to leave the *Granma*, trying to salvage some equipment.

Reaching the shore, the rebels realized they were in a huge mangrove swamp with water up to their knees or even their necks. Gnarled tree roots rose like an awesome obstacle course, vines and razor-like leaves slashed and beat their faces, and vast clouds of mosquitoes tried to devour them alive. The men's brand-new heavy boots slowed their advance; some boots and uniforms were so soaked and cut they began to come apart; rifles and ammunition became wet; equipment was lost.

Fidel led the way, the men constantly tripping over submerged tree trunks, falling down, picking each other up, leaning on one another, and somehow succeeding in moving ahead. One must attempt to cross this mangrove swamp oneself even to begin to understand the lung-bursting effort it represented.

At one stage Castro developed the paralyzing fear that they had landed on a coastal key and not on the [island of Cuba] and that they were trapped without means of escape by water. But soon one of the men, Luis Crespo, was able to climb a tree, and in the first light of the winter morning, discern land, palm trees, huts, and mountains in the distance. It took Castro's guerrilla army over two hours to reach firm ground across the mangrove swamp and a lagoon in the center of it, a distance of less than a mile in a straight line; it was a frightening and exhausting experience for them after a week at sea in the overcrowded little yacht. When they finally reached firm ground, they collapsed, panting, to rest. But Juan Manuel Marquez and seven other men were missing; they seemed to have been swallowed by the swamp, and their companions were immensely concerned about them.

Still, Fidel Castro had fulfilled his promise: he had returned to Cuba before the end of 1956, and now he was ready to open war on Batista. Like José Martí, who had landed at Playitas in the dark with a handful of companions sixty years earlier, Fidel Castro stood on the coast of Oriente on this December 2, anxious to liberate Cuba from her domestic enemies.

A Secret Meeting with Fidel Castro By H. L. Matthews[26]

On February 17, 1957, Herbert L. Matthews, a distinguished correspondent of The New York Times obtained a secret interview with Fidel Castro while he was still in his hiding place deep in the mountain vastness of Cuba's Sierra Maestra. At that time, as Matthews says, "For the Cuban people Fidel Castro was a myth, a legend, a hope, but not a reality." The Batista

This 1957 photograph, taken at a secret base, is believed to be the only existing one of Castro and members of his staff and troop commanders.

regime had announced that Fidel Castro was dead. United Press had even reported the place where he was buried.

Fidel Castro needed publicity desperately. Without a press he was only a hunted outlaw whom most Cubans thought dead. A foreign journalist was needed to make a reliable report: A journalist who could come to Cuba, obtain a story, and get out quickly to write it before the Batista regime could clamp down on the report under its tight censorship laws.

In the excerpt that follow, Matthews describes his interview with the young Castro. "I have never done a story that gave me more professional satisfaction," he writes. "There was a story to be got, a censorship broken. I got it and I did it—and it so happens that neither Cuba nor the United States is going to be the same again."

Late in the afternoon of February 15, 1957, Senor Castro's contact man got in touch with me in Havana with the news that the meeting was set for the following night in the Sierra and that Senor Castro and his staff would take a chance of coming a little way toward the edge of the range so that I would not have to do much climbing. There are no roads there, and where we were to meet, no horses could go.

To get from Havana to Oriente [more than five hundred miles away] on time meant driving all night and the next morning so as to be ready Saturday afternoon to start for the Sierra.

The plan worked out to get through the army's roadblocks in Oriente was as simple as it was effective. We took my wife along in the car as "camouflage." Cuba was at the height of the tourist season, and nothing could have looked more innocent than a middle-aged couple of American tourists driving down to Cuba's most beautiful and fertile province with some friends. The guards would take one look at my wife, hesitate a second, and wave us on with friendly smiles. If we were to be questioned, a story was prepared for them. If we were searched, the jig would be up.

In that way we reached the house of a sympathizer of Senor Castro outside the Sierra. There my wife was to stay amid the warm hospitality, and no questions asked. I got into the warm clothes I had purchased in Havana for "a fishing trip," warm for the cold night air of the mountains and dark for camouflage.

After nightfall I was taken to a certain house where

three youths who were going in with me had gathered. One of them was "One of the Eighty-Two," a proud phrase for the survivors of the original landing. I was to meet five or six of them. A courier who owned an open army-type Jeep joined us. His news was bad. A government patrol of four soldiers in a Jeep had placed itself on the very road we were to take to get near the point where we were to meet the Castro scouts at midnight. Moreover, there had been a heavy rain in the Sierra in the afternoon and the road was a morass. The others impressed on him that Fidel Castro wanted me in there at all costs and somehow it had to be done.

The courier agreed reluctantly. All across the plain of Oriente Province there are flatlands with sugar and rice plantations, and such farms have innumerable dirt roads. The courier knew every inch of the terrain and figured that by taking a very circuitous route he could bring us close enough. We had to go through one army roadblock, and beyond that would be the constant risk of army patrols, so we had to have a good story ready. I was to be an American sugar planter who could not speak a word of Spanish and who was going out to look over a plantation in a certain village. One of the youths who spoke English was my "interpreter." The others made up similar fictions.

Before leaving, one of the men showed me a wad of bills (the Cuban peso is exactly the same size as the United States dollar) amounting apparently to 400 pesos, which was being sent to Senor Castro. With a "rich" American planter it would be natural for the group to have the money if we were searched. It was interesting evidence that Fidel Castro paid for everything he took from the *guajiros,* or squatter farmers of the Sierra.

Our story convinced the army guard when he stopped us, although he looked dubious for a little while. Then came hours of driving, through sugarcane and rice fields, across rivers that only Jeeps could manage. One stretch, the courier said, was heavily patrolled by government troops, but we were lucky and saw none. Finally, after slithering through miles of mud, we could go no further.

It was then midnight, the time we were to meet Castro's scouts; but we had to walk some first, and it was hard going. At last we turned off the road and slid down a hillside to where a stream, dark brown under the nearly full moon, rushed its muddy way. One of the boys slipped and fell full length into the icy cold water. I waded through with the water almost up to my knees, and that was hard enough to do without falling. Fifty yards up the other slope was the meeting point.

The patrol was not there. Three of us waited while two of the men went back to see if we had missed the scouts somewhere, but in fifteen minutes they returned, frustrated. The courier suggested that we might move up a bit, and he led us ahead but obviously did not know where to go. Senor Castro's men have a characteristic signal that I was to hear incessantly—two low, soft, toneless whistles. One of our men kept trying it, but with no success. After a while we gave up. We had kept under cover at all times, for the moonlight was strong and we knew there were troops around us.

We stopped in a heavy clump of trees and bushes, dripping from the rain, the ground underfoot heavily matted, muddy, and soaked. There we sat for a whispered confab. The courier and another youth who had fought previously with Castro said they would go up the mountainside and see if they could find any of the rebel troops. Three of us were to wait, a rather agonizing wait of more than two hours, crouched in the mud, not daring to talk or move, trying to snatch a little sleep with our heads on our knees and annoyed maddeningly by the swarms of mosquitoes that were having the feast of their lives.

At last we heard a cautious, welcome double whistle. One of us replied in kind, and this had to be kept up for a while, like two groups meeting in a dense fog, until we got together. One of our party had found an advance patrol, and a scout came with him to lead us to an outpost in the mountains. The scout was a squatter from the hills, and he needed to know every inch of the land to take us as he did, swiftly and unerringly across the fields, up steep hills, floundering in the mud.

The ground leveled out blessedly at last and then dipped suddenly. The scout stopped and whistled cautiously. The return whistle came. There was a short parley and we were motioned on, sliding down into a heavy grove. The dripping leaves and boughs, the dense vegetation, the mud underfoot, the moonlight— all gave the impression of a tropical forest, more like Brazil than Cuba.

Senor Castro was encamped some distance away, and a soldier went to announce our arrival and ask whether he would join us or we should join him. Later he came back with the grateful news that we were to wait and Fidel would come along with the dawn. Someone gave me a few soda crackers, which tasted good. Someone else stretched a blanket on the ground, and it seemed a great luxury. It was too dark in the grove to see anything.

We spoke in the lowest possible whispers. One man told me how he had seen his brother's store wrecked and burned by government troops and his brother dragged out and executed. "I'd rather be here fighting for Fidel than anywhere in the world now," he said. There were two hours before dawn, and the blanket made it possible to sleep.

With the light I could see how young they all were. Senor Castro, according to his followers, is thirty, and that is old for the 26th of July Movement. It has a motley array of arms and uniforms, and even a few civilian suits. The rifles and the one machine gun I saw were all discarded American models.

Raúl Castro, Fidel's younger brother, slight and pleasant, came into the camp with others of the staff, and a few minutes later Fidel himself strode in. Taking him, as one would at first, by physique and personality, this was quite a man—a powerful six-footer, olive-skinned, full-faced, with a straggly beard. He was dressed in an olive-gray fatigue uniform and carried a rifle with a telescope sight, of which he was very proud. It seems his men have something more than fifty of these, and he said the soldiers feared them.

"We can pick them off at a thousand yards with these guns," he said.

After some general conversation we went to my blanket and sat down. Someone brought tomato juice, ham sandwiches made with crackers, and tins of coffee. In honor of the occasion, Senor Castro broke open a box of good Havana cigars, and for the next three hours we sat there while he talked. No one could talk above a whisper at any time. There were columns of government troops all around us, Senor Castro said, and their one hope was to catch him and his band.

The personality of the man is overpowering. It was easy to see that his men adored him and also to see why he has caught the imagination of the youth of Cuba all over the island. Here was an educated, dedicated fanatic, a man of ideals, of courage, and of remarkable qualities of leadership. As the story unfolded of how he had at first gathered the few remnants of the Eighty-Two around him; kept the government troops at bay while youths came in from other parts of Oriente as General Batista's counterterrorism aroused them; got arms and supplies and then began the series of raids and counterattacks of guerrilla warfare, one got a feeling that he is now invincible. Perhaps he isn't, but that is the faith he inspires in his followers.

They have had many fights and inflicted many

losses, Senor Castro said. Government planes came over and bombed every day; in fact, at nine sharp a plane did fly over. The troops took up positions; a man in a white shirt was hastily covered up. But the plane went on to bomb higher in the mountains. Castro is a great talker. His brown eyes flash; his intense face is pushed close to the listener and the whispering voice, as in a stage play, lends a vivid sense of drama.

"We have been fighting for seventy-nine days now and are stronger than ever," Senor Castro said. "The soldiers are fighting badly; their morale is low, and ours could not be higher. We are killing many, but when we take prisoners they are never shot. We question them, talk kindly to them, take their arms and equipment, and then set them free. I know that they are always arrested afterward and we heard some were shot as examples to the others, but they don't want to fight, and they don't know how to fight this kind of mountain warfare. We do.

"The Cuban people hear on the radio all about Algeria, but they never hear a word about us or read a word, thanks to the censorship. You will be the first to tell them. I have followers all over the island. All the best elements, especially all the youth, are with us. The Cuban people will stand anything but oppression."

I asked him about the report that he was going to declare revolutionary government in the Sierra. "Not yet," he replied. "The time is not ripe. I will make myself known at the opportune moment. It will have all the more effect for the delay, for now everybody is talking about us. We are sure of ourselves.

"There is no hurry. Cuba is in a state of war but Batista is hiding it. A dictatorship must show that it is omnipotent or it will fail; we are showing that it is impotent." The government, he said with some bitterness, is using arms furnished by the United States, not only against him but "against all the Cuban people."

"They have bazookas, mortars, machine guns, planes, and bombs," he said, "but we are safe in here in the Sierra; they must come and get us and they cannot."

Senor Castro speaks some English, but he preferred to speak in Spanish, which he did with extraordinary eloquence. His is a political mind rather than a military one. He has strong ideas of liberty, democracy, social justice, the need to restore the Constitution, to hold elections. He has strong ideas on economy too, but an economist would consider them weak.

The 26th of July Movement talks of nationalism, anti-colonialism, anti-imperialism. I asked Senor Castro about that. He answered, "You can be sure we have no animosity toward the United States and the American people.

"Above all," he said, "we are fighting for a democratic Cuba and an end to the dictatorship. We are not anti-military; that is why we let the soldier prisoners go. There is no hatred of the army as such, for we know the men are good and so are many of the officers.

"Batista has three thousand men in the field against us. I will not tell you how many we have, for obvious reasons. He works in columns of two hundred, we in groups of ten to forty, and we are winning. It is a battle against time, and time is on our side." To show that he deals fairly with the *guajiros* [squatters], he asked someone to bring "the cash." A soldier brought a bundle wrapped in dark brown cloth, which Senor Castro unrolled. There was a stack of peso bills at least a foot high, about $4,000, he said, adding that he had all the money he needed and could get more.

"Why should soldiers die for Batista for seventy-two dollars a month?" he asked. "When we win we will give them one hundred a month, and they will serve a free, democratic Cuba.

"I am always in the front line," he said, and others

confirmed this fact. Such being the case, the army might yet get him, but in present circumstances he seems almost invulnerable. "They never know where we are," he said, as the group rose to say good-bye, "but we always know where they are. You have taken quite a risk in coming here, but we have the whole area covered, and we will get you out safely."

They did. We plowed our way back through the muddy undergrowth in broad daylight, but always keeping under cover. The scout went like a homing pigeon through woods and across fields where there are no paths, straight to a farmer's house on the edge of the Sierra. There we hid in a back room while someone borrowed a horse and went for the Jeep, which had been under cover all night.

There was one roadblock to get through with an army guard so suspicious our hearts sank, but he let us through.

After that, shaved and looking once more like an American tourist, with my wife as camouflage, we had no trouble driving back through the roadblocks to safety and then on to Havana. So far as anyone knew, we had been away fishing for the weekend, and no one bothered us as we took the plane to New York.

THE DECISIVE MEETING
BY FULGENCIO BATISTA[27]

By the evening of December 31, 1959, Fulgencio Batista had come to realize that the military situation in Cuba was becoming untenable. If his presence in the country were to provoke the needless spilling of blood, he did not want to

Fulgencio Batista, president of Cuba from 1939 to 1959, was a brutal and oppressive dictator.

continue in power. He felt he must make one last effort to dominate the situation.

On the evening of December 31, he called a meeting of the country's military leaders.

In the excerpt that follows, Batista reports on his last meeting with the chiefs. He decided to resign.

After the meeting in the early morning hours, together with his wife and children, Batista flew to exile in the Dominican Republic.

Eventually he settled in Spain where he died.

The room where we met was cramped. It was two in the morning. The chiefs talked for a few moments and all agreed that it was impossible to continue the struggle.

The chief of the infantry division gave a résumé of his report of the exhausted condition of his command and the inability of most of his officers to urge a small group of tired men into battle. . . . The chief of the infantry district of Cabana explained that the fortress and the camp could count on no more than the minimum of troops necessary to keep them going; that his men were ready to sacrifice themselves, but that there were no reserves.

The Navy was more sound, although its ground units and personnel were working without relief. The chief was of the same opinion as the others. . . .

In conclusion, after disloyalties, surrenders, and treacheries, with only a scrap of the Army left, there was only a prospect of a mountain of bodies, with the horsemen of the Apocalypse seizing the remains of the Republic.

The resignation and surrender of the Government to a military junta was recommended. . . .

When we summoned the political leaders and officials who were asked to wait in the first floor salon, some had already departed. Anselmo Allegro was designated to pass on the Presidency to the oldest justice of the Supreme Court. Thus the Provisional Govern-

Cuban rebels in Santiago de Cuba pose for a photograph during the Revolution.

ment was formed in accordance with the provisions of the Constitution with General Eulogio Cantillo as chief of the Army.

The military leaders and civilians witnessed my resignation. I was answering the appeal to my patriotism which had once been made by the church, the industrialista, and the merchants, and was now being made by the military chiefs because they could not restore order.

In the document I implored God's favor to light the

way for the Cubans and to grant them the grace of living in peace and harmony.

In handing over the Government to my successor, I begged the people to be on their best behavior so that they would not be a victim of the hatreds and passions which had disgraced the Cuban family.

In the same way I urged all the members of the Armed Forces and agents of the law and order to obey their leaders under the authority of the new Government.

CASTRO'S VICTORY MARCH INTO HAVANA
BY NICHOLAS RIVERO[28]

When Fidel Castro and his company of revolutionaries overthrew the corrupt dictatorship of Fulgencio Batista, there was no question in anyone's mind of a Communist state. In his first statement after Batista had fled the country, Castro pledged that the aim of his revolutionary government was simply to restore freedom and constitutional guarantees of liberty.

In the excerpt that follows, Nicholas Rivero, later named press officer of the Foreign Ministry, sat in the reviewing stand when Castro made his victorious entrance into Havana. Castro was at the head of a caravan composed of three or four hundred barbudos (bearded ones), veterans of the Sierra Maestra, and units of the old Batista army detachments who had joined the victory parade along the route. More than fifteen thousand Batista soldiers, with their officers and their complete equipment, took part in this joyful victory march.

Fidel Castro (waving) arrives in Havana on January 8, 1959, to proclaim victory.

Castro made his victorious entrance into Havana on January 8, 1959. Never in the history of Cuba has anyone received such a tumultuous welcome. Crowds gathered along the entire route to the presidential palace, where Castro stopped to greet Provisional President Manuel Urrutia Lleo and his cabinet, then proceeded to Camp Columbia, symbol of the military might of Batista. I was in Camp Columbia in the reviewing stand when Castro arrived, and was sitting next to President Prio and Mr. and Mrs. Herbert Matthews of the *New York Times.*

Castro rode into the camp in the early evening hours carrying his famous telescopic rifle over his shoulder. Almost immediately he began to talk to the people of Cuba over a national television and radio hookup. As he spoke, someone in the crowd released two white doves, and one of them perched on Fidel's shoulder where it remained for about an hour, much to the delight of the crowd, which interpreted the incident as a good omen. With the four-hour Camp Columbia speech a new era began for the people of Cuba, who were blessedly unaware of what was in store for them.

It was my impression and that of many others who heard and saw him at Camp Columbia that evening that Fidel had that rare gift, which nature seems to bestow impartially on both good men and bad, of being able to sway popular feeling and emotions at will.

After the long dark years of dictatorship, Cuba again became a cheerful country. Havana, where I first met Castro under far different circumstances, was again a gay and relaxed city; the people were so joyful and no longer afraid to talk; the press, muzzled for so long, was again free. Castro's bearded, gun-toting partisans swarmed through the streets and the lobbies of the swank hotels, looking like brigands and acting like schoolchildren. Most of them were peasants from the back country, and to them Fidel was next to God. They were the humble heroes of a revolution they did not understand, and they were so imbued with the spirit of honesty of the revolution that no one could even buy them a meal or a drink. Such offers of hospitality were refused with the reply, "Thank you very much, but Fidel said no."

It was indeed a unique revolution—a disciplined one, and with great respect for public order. There were no police, but traffic moved smoothly and swiftly; crime was hard to find, perhaps, as they used to say, because all the crooks were in the Batista police force. In those days Fidel was indeed Mr. Cuba. Wherever he went—and he was all over Havana day and night—he was surrounded by hysterical crowds. When I accompanied him one evening through the luxurious lobby of the Havana Hilton Hotel, it took us hours to reach the door. He listened to anyone with a question to ask. He was exhausted and hoarse, but sustained by the inner energy of the genuine political leader.

VICE PRESIDENT RICHARD NIXON MEETS FIDEL CASTRO BY RICHARD NIXON[29]

In April 1959 Fidel Castro was invited to address the American Society of Newspaper Editors. He spent five days in Washington where he was widely received by people both in government and outside it.

Vice President Richard Nixon met with Fidel Castro for two hours in Nixon's office in the Capitol.

Richard Nixon's impression of Fidel Castro after their long talk follows.

My first impression of [Castro] was that he was simply an idealistic and impractical young man. He talked about primary government capital, arguing that plants licensed by government would serve Cuban interests better than private plants. He kept criticizing the American press, while I argued that he should learn from criticism both fair and unfair. I had the feeling that he would curtail press freedom in the future. But Castro told me, "You Americans are always so afraid— afraid of Communism, afraid of everything. You should be talking more about your own strengths and reasons why your system is superior to Communism or any other kind of dictatorship."

[From a memo written by Nixon immediately after their meeting]: I suggested at the outset that while I understood some reasonable time might elapse before it would be feasible to have elections, it would nevertheless be much better from his viewpoint if he were not to state so categorically that it would be as long as four years before elections would be held. . . . He went into considerable detail as he had in public with regard to the reasons for not holding elections, emphasizing particularly that "the people did not want elections because the elections in the past had produced bad government." It was also apparent that as far as his visit to the United States was concerned, his primary interest was not to get a change in the sugar quota or to get a government loan but to win support for his policies from American public opinion. . . . My own appraisal of him as a man is somewhat mixed. The one fact we can be sure of is that he has those indefinable qualities which make him a leader of men. Whatever we may think of him, he is going to be a great factor in the development of Cuba and very possibly in Latin American affairs generally. . . . He is either incredibly naive about Communism or under Communist discipline. My guess is the former. . . .

[Later the former American president mused over

the historic visit]: I've met many leaders. I've met Nkrumah and Sukarno, and they all are the same: they exude charisma; they exude, incidentally, sex appeal. It is not surprising to me to find they were ladies' men. All three would have been successful on the American scene. All three were demagogues. I could sense in private conversation how Castro could move an audience. . . . I felt his perception of the U.S. was distorted and that his anti-Americanism was virtually incurable. . . . I seldom get involved in like-dislike. . . . I respected him as a strong personality. I found him worthy of talking to. There aren't so many you find like this on the international scene. One thing worse than being wrong, it's being dull. He was wrong; he was not dull. He was someone I'd like to have on our side. Castro . . . was worth two hours.

THE BAY OF PIGS
BY HOWARD HUNT[30]

John F. Kennedy had been president of the United States only a few months when he was told that the Eisenhower administration had undertaken a secret plan to train and equip Cuban refugees to mount an invasion against their former homeland. The idea behind the plan was that the return of their countrymen would rouse the Cuban people to revolt against the Castro regime. President Kennedy doubted that the invasion plan would succeed. But when told that the Joint Chiefs of Staff had given their full approval to the idea, he finally agreed to go ahead with the invasion on one condition: that no American soldiers would be involved.

Howard Hunt, one of the Americans present in the war

room at the White House at the time of the invasion, reports on that heartbreaking night in 1961.

Coded Radio Message to Cuba

The following coded radio message was intended to deceive Castro about the nature of the Bay of Pigs invasion.

ALERT! ALERT! Look well at the rainbow. The first will rise very soon. Chico is in the house. Visit him. The sky is blue. . . . The fish is red.[31]

Many accounts have been written of the combat that took place at the Bay of Pigs, each different from one another, depending on the source and time. Obviously, descriptions supplied by brigade members who returned after long imprisonment are likely to be fuller and more reliable than those supplied by troops who escaped before the final collapse.

I was not on the beachhead, but I have talked with many Cubans who were. Rather than attempt to write what has been written before, it is enough to say that there were no cowards on the beach, aboard the assault ships, or in the air. There were few of us who did not pray for the brigade's deliverance.

Castro's fighters destroyed our B-26s that had been sent to clear the roads of Cuban tanks and artillery. Much of our armor, some ships, and landing craft were destroyed. Cut off from supplies, and under heavy pounding from the air, the brigade fought ferociously.

Throughout Monday, war room messages from the front turned from bad to worse. Frantic plans were made to get the B-26s over the battle area, but the long flight from Nicaragua allowed them only a few minutes of fighting time. The exiled pilots flew to the point of exhaustion, then blessed night fell and the brigade was given a measure of respite.

The fighting was now described as principally internal in character, the result of an uprising planned and triggered by exiles, rather than an organized invasion. A number of ships had fled, reducing the brigade's ability to communicate, and cutting off hope of further supplies.

According to Castro's own estimate, the brigade inflicted casualties at a rate of twenty to one.

On the diplomatic front Khrushchev [premier of the Soviet Union] had begun making warlike sounds— from a safe distance—and all this compounded the stress and confusion surrounding official Washington.

In the war room there was an air of bitter hopefulness. Nino Diaz [a Castro partisan who had defected] and his men, though not apprised of the beachhead situation, again flatly refused to land. Fearing outright mutiny, the ship's captain put to sea. Where he went nobody cared. Everyone looked to Bissell [chief of clandestine services] for a miracle. His ties to the White House were well known and authentic. Harassed beyond the limits of normal men, he played as many cards as he could: the administration was now shocked to its core. Earlier, while there was still daylight, three jets from the aircraft carrier *Boxer*, insignia painted out, were allowed a reconnaissance run over the Bay of Pigs. Their appearance briefly heartened the brigade, but in the war room we knew the strict limits of their authorization. . . .

Somehow the night passed.

In the morning one C-46 managed to land at Giron airstrip long enough to offload ammunition and communications equipment and pick up a few wounded. It was the only plane that landed in the battle zone, and it had been scheduled to fly in the provisional government.

Tuesday night the president was closeted with his principal advisers until ten o'clock, leaving the meeting long enough to put in an appearance at a formal White House ball. He returned to confer until two in the morning and when an exhausted Bissell entered the war room, we grouped hopefully around him.

The president's final concession was an hour's air cover over the beachhead in the early morning—from six to seven o'clock. The planes would come from the *Boxer* and were authorized to shoot anything hostile that moved. In that hour, scattered invasion ships were to move in and unload. Meanwhile, hopefully, Castro's remaining fighters would be shot down.

This strange compromise electrified us, and at once all hands returned to work exultant and refreshed. I tried not to read the pitiful messages that trickled in from San Roman [leader of the invasion brigade], telling myself that the next day would turn the tide. Encouraging words were flashed to the beachhead, our maritime operations officers began rounding up the surviving ships, and Colonel George ordered what was left of our air force to arm against Russian tanks and artillery. I phoned Bender to give him the joyful news, and he nearly broke down. Then I prepared a new war communiqué stressing the use of Russian weapons against Cuban patriots.

Our spirits bursting high, we gulped quarts of coffee as compliance began coming back from the ships. The sky lightened; we checked our watches and waited for the hour of deliverance.

Then from San Roman came the incredible report that our B-26s had arrived only to be shot down. The *Boxer*'s jets appeared over Giron while their wreckage was still burning. By some incalculable mischance the timing had been fouled up. By then we had run out of time, aircraft, and men. The invasion was over. Wading into the water that afternoon, San Roman sent a final bitter message: "I have nothing to fight with. I am taking to the woods. I cannot wait for you."

Silently we wept. Never before had I seen a room filled with men in tears. I was sure Artime [leader of the brigade] and all the others were dead, and I blamed myself for having been party to their betrayal.

Our daze lasted until we learned that the White House had ordered task force destroyers to move in and pick up wounded and stragglers, men in boats and on rafts, wounded clinging to bits of wreckage.

A reconnaissance jet reported seeing a few survivors in the water, but on the beachhead only vultures moved.

I was sick of lying and deception, heartsick over political compromise and military defeat. I went home.

That night, laced through my broken sleep were the words of Sir Winston Churchill: "I am not sure I should have dared to start the invasion: but I am sure I should not have dared to stop."

THE BITTER LESSON
BY JAMES MONAHAN
AND KENNETH GILMORE[32]

Some nine months after the Bay of Pigs disaster, the survivors of that tragic invasion attempt returned to the United States, ransomed with $60 million worth of pharmaceuticals and foodstuffs.

José San Roman, commander of the ill-fated brigade, spoke for his companions: "We don't know how or in what form the

Christmas week 1962 in Miami was emblazoned by more than yuletide decorations and bright skies. Beginning on Christmas Eve, the 1,113 men of the Brigade 2506, who had been Fidel Castro's captives since April 1961, were returned to freedom in Florida, ransomed by some $60 million worth of pharmaceuticals and foodstuffs, a partial expiation for the U.S. blunders in the Bay of Pigs tragedy. To the last man, they were proud, undefeated warriors, who resisted the evils of Communist brainwashing and survived the rigors and deprivation of Castro's jails. They were also firm in their determination to fight again for Cuba's freedom.

Manuel Artime, civilian leader of the Liberation Army, declared: "We will fight again. We have given our word to our dead, to the Cuban people, and to the Free World that we will liberate Cuba or die in the attempt."

On Saturday, December 29, 35,000 Cubans filled the grandstand of Miami's Orange Bowl as President Kennedy reviewed the officers and men of the Brigade of 2506 and accepted its proudest possession, the brigade colors. "I want to express my great appreciation to the Brigade," the president said, "for making the United States the custodian of this flag. I can assure you that this flag will be returned to the brigade in a free Havana."

Said José San Roman, commander of the brigade,

A billboard in the resort town of Giron expresses the pride Cubans felt after dealing U.S.-backed forces a resounding defeat in the 1961 Bay of Pigs invasion. The sign reads, "Giron Beach [the Cuban name for the battle of the Bay of Pigs], the first defeat of imperialism in Latin America."

"We don't know how or in what form the opportunity will come for us to fight in the cause of Cuba. Whenever, however, wherever, in whatever honorable form it may come, we will do what we can to be better prepared to meet and complete our mission."

Liberation, to most Cubans, was only a matter of time. José Ignacio Rasco expressed the solemn, hopeful, long-range view. "We are aware," he said, "that our struggle will only begin with the liberation of Cuba. We will face enormous tasks in rebuilding our

Communist-wrecked government with democratic government, with democratic safeguards, and perhaps the greatest task of all—in rehabilitating a generation of Cubans whose minds have been perverted by Communist indoctrination.

"We have learned some bitter lessons, and we have more to learn still. But I think the free people of the Western Hemisphere have much to learn with us, both from our sad experience and our future actions. The most solemn lesson, I believe is this: Never again must the free people anywhere in the Americas say, as we said in Cuba, 'Communism can never happen here.'"

THE CARDENAS AFFAIR
BY AN EYEWITNESS[33]

Fidel Castro never made the mistake of undervaluing popular protests against him. He knew that a handful of rebels supported by an angry crowd had succeeded in overturning the Batista government. When he heard of the demonstration at Cárdenas, he decided to intervene promptly with a show of force, even sending President Dorticós to the revolutionary meeting that followed the spontaneous demonstration. His prompt repression of the Cárdenas incident in 1962 was designed to convince the Cuban people that he was ready to stamp out by force any manifestation of popular revolt.

For many weeks, even months, there had been much grumbling and some noisy protests among the housewives who queued up in front of the various shops and markets with their ration cards, waiting to buy food that was in short supply or never to be had. At first this was tempered by jokes and laughter, like taunting the militia men and making loud remarks about the well-fed Russians and Poles and the fat Chinese. But by mid-June there was less laughter; tempers were getting short, there were more arguments, fights, and outcries.

On this Saturday morning [June 16, 1962] the downtown area of Cárdenas was crowded with as many men—farmers, factory laborers, dockworkers—as women. The trouble started, innocently enough, with a peaceful procession of women. I saw them coming down the side street toward the Parque de Colón. Most of them carried pots, pans, and other cooking utensils as symbols of their status as housewives, and all carried their "deceivers" [ration cards] which they waved in the air. The destination was the town hall, where they planned to register a peaceful protest against the food shortage and, after that, to assemble at the Church of the Purisma Concepción.

However, as the procession passed the market surrounding the Plaza del Mercado, many people deserted the long food lines and joined the marchers. Some of the women began beating pots and pans, and the others took up the beat in unison. Then the chanting began: "We are hungry!" "Fidel, we want food!" "Cuba, si! Comunismo, no!" Soon the crowds got bolder: "Down with communism! Down with Castro!"

The commotion drew crowds from the side streets, and long before the housewives' procession was lost in the mob, the streets were jammed for blocks around. When police and militia tried to halt the mob at crossings, they were practically trampled underfoot. They couldn't possibly break up or control the crowds.

Groups of communist thugs recruited from the dockworkers' union came to the assistance of the police, and fighting started. At one point a huge army truck equipped with a loudspeaker tried to plow through the mass of people. The voice over the loud-speaker was saying: "Food is coming. . . . Fidel has said that food is on the way. . . . Patrio o muerto! Venceremos!" (Fatherland or death! We will win!) The mob stopped the truck, beat up the driver, and made the other fellow shout over the loudspeaker, "Down with communism!"

The rioting went on for hours, but word must have been flashed to Havana very early, because by after-noon the troops began to arrive. These were units 20–28 of the Revolutionary Army and three battalions from Division 10, which was garrisoned in Matanzas. The roads leading into Cárdenas were lined with So-viet tanks, weapons carriers, field artillery, antiaircraft guns, and truckload after truckload of armed soldiers. Two Soviet Kronstadt sub chasers appeared in the har-bor with deck guns manned and ready for action. A formation of MiG fighters flew back and forth over the city for the rest of the day. President Dorticós arrived with the troops from Havana. A rostrum was set up in the Esplanada in front of the museum library, and be-hind it they set up an enormous sign reading, "Social-ism is peace." "It was truly amazing how thoroughly this revolutionary mass meeting was organized in such a short time."

Television carried nearly every aspect of the Cár-denas uprising throughout Cuba—mob scenes, the military show of force, and finally the long, impas-sioned speech by Dorticós.

Dorticós boasted, threatened, cajoled, and did his best to make it appear that the uprising was the work of a counterrevolutionary minority and that it had been put down by a majority which was loyal to the regime. But he did not hesitate to remind his vast tele-vision audience that the stern countermeasures taken in Cárdenas were intended as a lesson to the rest of Cuba.

"This afternoon," he said, "has afforded a vigorous spectacle that demonstrates, on a single occasion, the force that sustains our revolution and also serves as a warning to our enemies with this modest example of the military strength of people under arms . . . our enemies forget one fact; revolutionaries are tempered and they grow in stature in struggle and combat. Our enemies forget that this is a revolution forged out of heroic efforts and that we will always respond [with force] when faced with enemy aggression. . . . If another provocation would be tried here, the entire population of Cárdenas would respond with even more vigor and mettle!" (Here the Communists in the crowd set up the cry "*Pardon*! Pardon!")

Dorticós admitted that things were far from rosy, but he blamed everything on the imperialists and counterrevolutionaries. "It is a fact," he said, "that we are facing difficulties and shortages. [But] in the first place, these shortages are a result of imperialist economic aggression. In the second place, the progressive increase in our people's consuming capacity had exceeded our present production capacity. It is also true that some of our mistakes and shortcomings have aggravated the situation. The enemy tries to take advantage of these material conditions and uses them to promote popular discontent. . . .

"These shortages and sacrifices today are the price we must pay in order to attain tomorrow's abundance. We can overcome them only by our own work and our own efforts. Sacrifice tempers character, and we are a people accustomed to sacrifices. Workers and peasants, let us merge ourselves in a firm alliance! Let us construct the fatherland for workers and peasants! Let us smash with the full weight of our revolutionary people these parasites of the counterrevolution! . . . . Do not allow these parasites to get away with another single act of provocation. We will not have to use these tanks or machine guns on them. Your efforts alone are enough to crush them, Comrades! If they repeat their provocations, then the people will crush them in the streets, or our armed forces will be here!"

Reports from various parts of the island indicate that most Cubans were shocked and horrified by the televised spectacle.

Padre Humberto, who watched it in Santiago de Cuba, comments: "This was either an act of desperation or incredible stupidity on Castro's part. We in the underground, of course, were delighted, because the television show from Cárdenas only fanned the flames of the peoples' resentment. Why, for instance, had they chosen Cárdenas for this demonstration—Cárdenas, the historical 'Flag City of Cuba,' where the first banner of Cuban freedom was raised more than a century ago? Did Fidel Castro think that, in three years of terror, he had erased from our minds all pride in our historic past?"

Alonso León, the former soap salesman, now a seriously ill and prematurely old man living near Havana, watched the spectacle on television and was reminded of Hungary, a reaction which is mentioned by many Cubans.

"The city of Cárdenas," he says, "was Cuba's Little Budapest—less bloody, perhaps, but also not as final. Cuba's bloody Budapest still may come."

JOHN F. KENNEDY'S ADDRESS TO THE AMERICAN PEOPLE ON THE SOVIET MISSILE BASES IN CUBA[34]

During October 1962 the U.S. government learned that the Soviets were sending missiles to Cuba and that a general arms buildup was under way. On October 22 a determined

MEDIUM RANGE BALLISTIC MISSILE BASE IN CUBA

ERECTOR ON LAUNCH PAD

MISSILE READY BLDGS

OXIDIZER VEHICLES

PROB HYDROGEN PEROXIDE TANKS

MISSILE READY BLDGS

FUELING VEHICLES

TENTS

ERECTOR ON LAUNCH PAD

MISSILE ON TRAILER

This photograph, taken on October 23, 1962, by a U.S. reconnaissance plane, shows the construction of a Soviet nuclear-missile site in Cuba. The United States responded swiftly to the Soviet military buildup in Cuba, eventually persuading the Soviets to withdraw their nuclear missiles.

President Kennedy alerted the American people to the dangerous situation. This eloquent and forceful speech set off a chain of events that persuaded Khrushchev to withdraw his ships and return them to Russia with their dangerous load of missiles.

Good evening, my fellow citizens.

This government, as promised, has maintained the closest surveillance of the Soviet military buildup on the island of Cuba. Within the past week, unmistakable evidence has established the fact that a series of offensive missile sites is now in preparation on that imprisoned island. The purpose of these bases can be none other than to provide a nuclear strike capability against the Western Hemisphere.

Upon receiving the first preliminary hard information of this nature last Thursday morning at 9:00 A.M., I directed that our surveillance be stepped up. And having now confirmed and completed our evaluation of the evidence and our decision on a course of action, this government feels obliged to report this new crisis to you in full detail.

The characteristics of these new missile sites indicate two distinct types of installations. Several of them include medium-range ballistic missiles, capable of carrying a nuclear warhead for a distance of more than one thousand nautical miles. Each of these missiles, in short, is capable of striking Washington, D.C., the Panama Canal, Cape Canaveral, Mexico City, or any other city in Central America or in the Caribbean area.

Additional sites not yet completed appear to be designed for intermediate-range ballistic missiles—capable of traveling more than twice as far—and thus capable of striking most of the major cities in the Western Hemisphere, ranging as far north as Hudson's Bay, Canada, and as far south as Lima, Peru. In addition, jet bombers, capable of carrying nuclear weapons, are now being uncrated and assembled on Cuba, while the necessary air bases are being prepared.

The urgent transformation of Cuba into an important strategic base—by the presence of these large, long-range, and clearly offensive weapons of sudden mass destruction—constitutes an explicit threat to the peace and security of all the Americas, in flagrant and deliberate defiance of the Rio Pact of 1947, the traditions of this nation and hemisphere, the joint resolution of the 87th Congress, the Charter of the United Nations, and my own public warnings to the Soviets on September 4 and 13. This action also contradicts the repeated assurances of Soviet spokesmen, both publicly and privately delivered, that the arms buildup in Cuba would retain its original defensive character and that the Soviet Union had no need or desire to station strategic weapons on the territory of any other nation.

The size of this undertaking makes clear that it had been planned some months ago. Yet only last month, after I had made clear the distinction between any introduction of ground-to-ground missiles and the existence of antiaircraft missiles, the Soviet government publicly stated on September 11 that "the armaments and military equipment sent to Cuba are designed exclusively for defensive purposes," that "there is no need to search for sites for them beyond the boundaries of the Soviet Union." That statement was false.

Only last Thursday, as evidence of this rapid offensive buildup was already in my hand, Soviet Foreign Minister Gromyko told me in my office that he was instructed to make it clear once again, as he said his government had already done, that Soviet assistance to Cuba "pursued solely the purpose of contributing to the defense capabilities of Cuba," that "training by

President John Kennedy addresses a U.S. television audience on November 2, 1962, to keep the public abreast of events during the Cuban Missile Crisis.

Soviet specialists of Cuban nationals in handling defensive armaments was by no means offensive," and that "if it were otherwise, the Soviet government would never become involved in rendering such assistance." That statement was also false.

Neither the United States of America nor the world community of nations can tolerate this on the part of any nation, large or small. We no longer live in a world where only the actual firing of weapons represents a sufficient challenge to a nation's security or constitutes a maximum peril. Nuclear weapons are so destructive and ballistic missiles are so swift that any substantially increased possibility of their use or any sudden change in their development may well be regarded as a definite threat to the peace.

For many years, both the Soviet Union and the United States—recognizing this fact—have deployed strategic nuclear weapons with great care, never upsetting the precarious status quo, which ensured that these weapons would not be used in the absence of some vital challenge. Our own strategic missiles have never been transferred to the territory of any other nation under a cloak of secrecy and deception; and our history—unlike that of the Soviets since World War II—demonstrates that we have no desire to dominate or conquer any other nation or impose our system upon its people. Nevertheless, American citizens have become adjusted to living daily on the bull's-eye of Soviet missiles located inside the USSR or in submarines. In that sense, missiles in Cuba add to an already clear and present danger—although, it should be noted, the nations of Latin America have never previously been subjected to a potential nuclear threat.

But this secret, swift, and extraordinary buildup of Communist missiles in an area well known to have a special and historical relationship to the United States and the nations of the Western Hemisphere, in violation of Soviet assurances and in defiance of American and hemispheric policy, this sudden clandestine decision to station strategic weapons for the first time outside of Soviet soil is a deliberately provocative and unjustified change in the status quo which cannot be accepted by this country if our courage and our commitments are ever to be trusted again by either friend or foe.

The 1920s taught us a clear lesson: aggressive conduct, if allowed to grow unchecked and unchallenged, ultimately leads to war. This nation is opposed to war. We are also true to our word. Our unswerving objective, therefore, must be to prevent the use of these missiles against this or any other country and to secure their withdrawal or elimination from the Western Hemisphere.

Our policy has been one of patience and restraint, as befits a peaceful and powerful nation which leads a worldwide alliance. We have been determined not to be diverted from our central concerns by mere irritants and fanatics. But now further action is required—and it is under way; and these actions may only be the beginning. We will not prematurely or unnaturally risk the costs of worldwide nuclear war in which even the fruits of victory would be ashes in our mouth, but neither will we shrink from that risk at any time it must be faced.

Acting, therefore, in the defense of our own security and that of the entire Western Hemisphere, and under the authority entrusted to me by the Constitution as endorsed by the resolution of the Congress, I have directed that the following initial steps be taken immediately:

First: To halt this offensive buildup, a strict quarantine on all offensive military equipment under shipment to Cuba is being initiated. All ships of any kind bound for Cuba, from whatever nation or port, will, if found to contain cargoes of offensive weapons be turned back. This quarantine will be extended, if needed, to other types of cargoes and carriers. We are not at this time, however, denying the necessities of life as the Soviets attempted to do in the Berlin blockade of 1948.

Second: I have directed the continued and increased surveillance of Cuba and its military buildup. The foreign ministers of the OAS [Organization of

American States] in their communication of October 6 rejected secrecy on such matters in this hemisphere. Should these offensive military preparations continue, thus increasing the threat to the hemisphere, further action will be justified. I have directed the armed forces to prepare for any eventualities; and I trust that in the interest of both the Cuban people and the Soviet technicians at these sites the hazards to all concerned of continuing the threat will be recognized.

Third: It shall be the policy of this nation to regard any nuclear missile launched from Cuba against any nation in the Western Hemisphere an attack by the Soviet Union on the United States requiring full retaliatory response upon the Soviet Union.

Fourth: As a necessary military precaution, I have reinforced our base at Guantánamo, evacuated today the dependents of our personnel there, and ordered additional military units to stand by on an alert basis.

Fifth: We are calling tonight for an immediate meeting of the Organ of Consultation under the Organization of American States to consider this threat to hemispheric security and to invoke Articles 6 and 8 of the Rio Treaty in support of all necessary action. The United Nations Charter allows for regional security arrangements, and the nations of this hemisphere decided long ago against military presence of outside powers. Our other allies around the world have been also alerted.

Sixth: Under the Charter of the United Nations we are asking tonight that an emergency meeting of the Security Council be invoked without delay to take action against this latest Soviet threat to world peace. Our resolution will call for the prompt dismantling and withdrawal of all offensive weapons in Cuba, under the supervision of the U.N. observers, before quarantine can be lifted.

Seventh and finally: I call upon Chairman Khrushchev to halt and eliminate this clandestine, reckless, and provocative threat to world peace and to stable relations between our two nations. I call upon him further to abandon this course of world domination and to join in an historic effort to end the perilous arms race and to transform the history of man. He has an opportunity now to move the world back from the abyss of destruction by returning to his government's own word that it had no need to station missiles outside its own territory and withdrawing these weapons from Cuba, by refraining from any action which will widen or deepen the present crisis, and then by participating in a search for peaceful and permanent solutions.

The nation is prepared to present its case against this Soviet threat to peace, and our own proposals for a peaceful world at any time and in any forum—in the OAS, in the United Nations, or in any other meeting that could be useful without limiting our freedom of action. We have in the past made strenuous efforts to limit the spread of nuclear weapons. We have proposed the elimination of all arms and military bases in a fair and effective disarmament treaty. We are prepared to discuss new proposals for the removal of tensions on both sides, including the possibility of a genuinely independent Cuba, free to determine its own destiny. We have no wish to go to war with the Soviet Union, for we are a peaceful people who desire to live in peace with all other people.

But it is difficult to settle or even discuss these problems in an atmosphere of intimidation. That is why this latest Soviet threat—or any other threat which is made either independently or in response to our actions this week—must and will be met with determination. Any hostile move anywhere in the world against the safety and freedom of peoples to whom we are committed—including in particular the brave people of West Berlin—will be met by whatever action is needed.

Finally I want to say a few words to the captive people of Cuba, to whom this speech is directly carried by special radio facilities. I speak to you as a friend, as one who knows of your deep attachment to your fatherland, as one who shares your aspirations for liberty and justice for all. And I have watched with deep sorrow how your nationalist revolution was betrayed and how your fatherland fell under foreign domination. Now your leaders are no longer Cuban leaders inspired by Cuban ideals. They are puppets and agents of an international conspiracy which has turned Cuba against your friends and neighbors in the Americas— and turned it into the first Latin American country to become a target for nuclear war, the first Latin American country to have these weapons on its soil.

These new weapons are not in your interest. They contribute nothing to your peace and well-being. They can only undermine it. But this country has no wish to cause you to suffer or to impose any system upon you. We know your lives and land are being used as pawns by those who deny you freedom.

Many times in the past, the Cuban people have risen to throw out tyrants who destroyed their liberty. And I have no doubt that most Cubans today look forward to the time when they will be truly free—free from foreign domination, free to choose their own leaders, free to select their own system, free to own their own land, free to speak and write and worship without fear or degradation. And then shall Cuba be welcomed back to the society of free nations and to the associations of this hemisphere.

My fellow citizens, let no one doubt that this is a difficult and dangerous effort on which we have set out. No one can foresee precisely what course it will take or what costs or casualties will be incurred. Many months in which both our will and our patience will be tested—months in which many threats and denunciations will keep us aware of our danger. But the greatest danger of all would be to do nothing.

The path we have chosen for the present is full of hazards, as all paths are, but it is the one most consistent with our character and courage as a nation and our commitments around the world. The cost of freedom is always high—but Americans have always paid it. And one path we shall never choose is the path of surrender or submission.

Our goal is not the victory of insight but the vindication of right—not peace at the expense of freedom, but both peace and freedom, here in this hemisphere and, we hope, around the world. God willing that goal will be achieved.

THE SUGAR HARVEST
BY PEDRO MANUEL BARERA
WITH ROBERT FUENTES[35]

The growing and selling of sugarcane is the foundation on which the Cuban economy is based. By far the greatest percentage of the crop is purchased by the United States. The cane planted the previous year is cut and processed industrially to produce sugar, in a period of feverish activity that lasts from five to six months.

Before the Castro revolution, sugarcane was cut solely with machetes, by experienced cutters who normally worked in pairs or groups of three. With the coming of the revolution, many of these cutters turned to other work. The result was a labor crisis in the cane fields. The revolution called upon the nation's trade unions, students, and soldiers for "voluntary brigades" of cane-cutters to come to the rescue.

This year and every year these voluntary brigades are organized during the harvest. Meanwhile the government, with

Time stands still in the cane fields. Inside the field the cane dominates; later man will have his day, but a doubt always remains. Next year cane will grow again and you will once again bend your back before it. The older men speak of the cane with respect: "The cane is hard," and they show their battered hands.

They call me Babalu. I carry coffee to the cane field and pass it out. My real name is Pedro Manuel Barera but I like Babalu better.

The second day is decisive. Whoever stays in the cane after the second day can last the whole harvest. Every pain on earth blooms the second day. Your hand won't close, the cane refuses to fall with one blow of the machete, and you have to hit it again and again, your waist aches and you don't know whether to lie down or stay on your feet.

Maceo is the political instructor of the brigade. Everybody calls him Commissar in the style of the Soviet army or of the Spanish Civil War. For Maceo the harvest is hard. "I never cut cane before, and I was to set an example here. I am fine now. A real cane-cutter. The doctor said I had a problem in my vertebral column, but he doesn't know what he's talking about."

Euspicio's machete glanced off and injured his right foot. El Jabao was hit in the face and eyes by the cane. In the cane field one doesn't think. Just grab three, four, bend and cut. Throw them on the pile, and grab three more, cut, throw, this sun, this sweat, this cane. Cut four and throw them, start a new clump.

When you learn of the injured you think, I'm too careless. I have to think about what I'm doing. But then the cane makes you forget everything. In the cane fields, the ferrets eat the rats and suck the sweetest cane. The herons eat the lizards, the worms, and the toads. The men notice the smell of sweat from the bodies of others but not from their own. Sleep, the dream is always left in the air, sleep and cut; cutting there is always plenty of, but sleep no. Sleepiness has neither beginning nor end; it is a long chain from the moment one arrives at the camp until the last day. One awakens automatically at four in the morning looking at the black roof without really seeing it. Straighten the blanket, warm yourself in it, and deep inside, hope there is no moon, that it is too dark, and they won't let us go so early to the cane field. Hope lasts a few minutes, but then someone shouts: "Rise and shine!" The shout grates down to the bone, and no one replies.

Get out of bed and say nothing, only the necessary words: "Hand me the soap, loan me the towel." Some are still sleeping and the shout comes again: "Artillerymen, rise and shine!" The laggards reply, "Coming, coming." They have no desire to get up, stealing a few more minutes in bed, in the warmth of the blanket, and who knows? "Maybe they'll forget all about me and I can sleep the whole morning for a change."

But they are gotten up one by one. "All right, all right, up and at 'em." One's clothes are cold and the boots hard. The hot coffee feels painful on an empty stomach. Then the truck and the road and nobody speaks. Finally there they stand before us, covered with sticky dew that splatters and makes the clothing colder.

Gloves get hardened, stiff from sweat and dirt. At midday you would like to sleep, but sometimes it is impossible with sweat running down your face and chest. This is war. The artillerymen resemble ants swarming over the cane fields. After two clumps of cane you lose the notion of why you are working. You earn no pay from it; the work is mechanical. Cane-cutter, loader, sugar mill, economy, revolution—all is forgotten. Only the cane remains before you and the sun above: the cane, that long, green stalk that twists and struggles not to be cut. Then everything seems stupid.

It's knowing how to take four canes at a time and throw them with precision on the pile and cutting faultlessly: a cut and all in one blow, cutting right down to the earth and using the mocha instead of the machete. The mocha is heavier, and the body makes less effort. The cane-cutter despises the thin cane covered with husk that has no weight and twists around the others; he prefers the thick, sweet, erect. If it's very bad cane we set fire to it and get rid of the husks. Since I have a big nose, it gets covered with soot in the burned cane and the fellows ask me, "Do you smell the cane or cut it?"

In the early morning you cut the cane blindly by instinct. We did it a million times. The cane-cutters threw themselves into cutting and fell unconscious on the cane. "The pain was so intense we sank our hands into buckets of cold water," says Pititi. "I still can't close my hands." Tio Papo ached so much in his muscles that he sobbed and cut at the same time. I awaken at four in the morning and always see Euspicio looking outside, with his tall body outlined in the frame of light made by the open door. "He has the face of a haunted man," Bernardo said to me. "One morning I got up before he did and looked outside. All was dark, and the only thing to be seen was the moon wrapped in mist."

A mirror is hung on the central pole of the barracks. It is the only one the brigade has. Each time one of us passes it, he looks at his reflection and caresses his beard. Brotherhood is a necessity. It is important that Engana lend his pistol to those who are going out on pass, that Mojena leave his money on his bunk "and let the boys take what they need," that the cook Beltran try to please everyone's taste. "Cata doesn't drink milk so I send him refreshments," [the cook says]. "Mello has a big stomach so I give him more." That's important. It isn't a written order, but it's the first law of the brigade.

I am going now, leaving the brigade. I wave good-bye to the brigade at breakfast; they present me with a mocha [coffee]. As I leave they raise their left fists in farewell. I, too, raise mine. Farewells of revolutionaries must be sadder than farewells of others. Revolutionaries have to say farewell many times. I look back and can no longer recognize Maceo and Mangana and Domingo from the cane and the mochas. I know they are there. They are also with me, name by name, in these notes that are now ended.

FAREWELL LETTER
TO FIDEL CASTRO
BY ERNESTO "CHE" GUEVARA[36]

Ernesto "Che" Guevara was born in Rosario, Argentina, on June 14, 1928. As a child he suffered so badly from asthma that he was forced to live in a small mountain town not far from Rosario. Even as a boy he was a passionate reader; history and sociology were his favorite subjects. Through his reading he came under the influence of the Chilean Communist poet and diplomat, Pablo Neruda. At nineteen he entered medical school at the University of Buenos Aires, graduating in 1953 with a degree of doctor of medicine and surgery.

Ernesto "Che" Guevara became good friends with Fidel Castro in Mexico. Together they planned Batista's overthrow. A passionate believer in guerrilla warfare, he was shot to death in 1967 in Bolivia while part of a band of guerrillas.

After medical school Guevara moved to Guatemala and lived there until Guatemala became involved in war; then he settled in Mexico. There Guevara met the Castro brothers, Fidel and Raúl. At the time, Fidel was planning his expedition against the Cuban dictator Fulgencio Batista. The two young men became fast friends ("Che" means "Pal"), and from that time on, Guevara was one of Fidel's most trusted advisers and comrades-in-arms.

A passionate believer in guerrilla warfare, Guevara had gone to Bolivia in the summer of 1966 to lead a guerrilla group in the region of Santa Cruz. On October 8, 1967, the small band of guerrillas was attacked by a detachment of the Bolivian army and Guevara was captured after being wounded. He was shot to death soon afterward.

The letter that follows is Che's farewell to his friend Fidel. It was read by Castro during the televised ceremony of the presentation of the newly established Central Communist party of Cuba. Castro explained that the letter had been delivered to him months earlier and that Guevara had left the timing of the disclosure to Castro's discretion. He had delayed making it public out of concern for his friend's security.

When Guevara's death was announced, Castro delivered a tribute to his friend in the Plaza de la Revolución in Havana. "He was," Castro said, "one of the dearest, the most admired, the most beloved, and without a doubt, the most extraordinary of our revolutionary comrades."

For Fidel Castro personally, Che Guevara's death meant not only the death of a valued comrade-in-arms but the loss of a much loved friend.

Fidel:

At this moment I remember many things—When I met you in Maria Antonia's house, when you suggested my coming, all the tensions involved in the preparations.

One day they asked who should be notified in case of death, and the real possibility of that fact affected us all. Later we knew that it was true, that in revolution (if it is a real one) one wins or dies. Many comrades fell along the way to victory. Today everything is less dramatic, because we are more mature. But the fact is repeated. I feel that I have fulfilled the part of my duty that tied me to the Cuban Revolution . . . and I say good-bye to you, the comrades, your people, who are already mine.

I formally renounce my positions in the national leadership of the party, my post as minister, my rank of major, and my Cuban citizenship. Nothing legal binds me to Cuba. The only ties are of another nature—those which cannot be broken as appointments can.

Recalling my past life, I believe I have worked with sufficient honor and dedication to consolidate the revolutionary triumph. My only serious failing was not having confided more in you from the first moments in the Sierra Maestra, and not having understood quickly enough your qualities as a leader and a revolutionary. I have lived magnificent days, and I felt at your side the pride of belonging to our people in the brilliant yet sad days of the Caribbean crisis.

Seldom has a statesman been more brilliant than you in those days. I am also proud of having followed you without hesitation, identified with your ways of thinking, and of seeing and appraising dangers and also principles.

Other nations of the world call for my modest efforts. I can do that which is denied you because of your responsibility as the head of Cuba, and the time has come for us to part.

I want it known that I do it with mixed feelings of joy and sorrow: I leave here the purest of my hopes as a builder, and the dearest of those I love. And I leave a people who received me as a son. That wounds me deeply. I carry to new battlefronts the faith that you taught me, the revolutionary spirit of my people, the feeling of fulfilling the most sacred of duties: to fight against imperialism wherever it may be. This comforts and heals the deepest wounds.

I state once more that I free Cuba from any responsibility, except that which stems from its example. If my final hour finds me under other skies, my last thought will be of this people and especially of you. I am thankful for your teaching, your example, and I will try to be faithful to the final consequences of my acts.

I have always been identified with the foreign policy of our revolution, and I will continue to be. Wherever I am, I will feel the responsibility of being a Cuban revolutionary, and as such I shall behave. I am not sorry that I leave my children and my wife nothing material. I am happy it is that way. I ask nothing for them, as I know the state will provide enough for their expenses and education.

I would like to say much to you and to our people, but I feel it is not necessary. Words cannot express what I would want them to, and I don't think it's worthwhile to bandy phrases.

Ever onward to victory! Our country or death!

I embrace you with all my revolutionary fervor.

Che

NIKITA KHRUSHCHEV SPEAKS ABOUT THE CUBAN MISSILE CRISIS OF 1962[37]

Five years after the missile incident of 1962, in a television broadcast, Nikita Khrushchev, the premier of the former USSR, discussed the failed American-sponsored invasion of Cuban exiles from Miami at Cuba's Bay of Pigs.

Khrushchev was philosophical about the whole sequence of events that began with the Cuban missile crisis. "It is difficult to say what might have happened," he said, "if we had not

This aerial photograph of the Soviet ship Fizik Kurchatov shows six canvas-covered missile transporters on its deck. Pressure from the United States forced Soviet premier Nikita Khrushchev to recall the missiles from Cuba.

When Cuba was invaded, April 1961, Bay of Pigs, I
heard about it on the radio, but we didn't know who
had done the invading, whether it was the Cuban
counterrevolutionaries or America's. But all the same,
we thought that no matter under what disguise, the invasion must be taking place with American participa-
tion. I would like to explain the situation leading up to
the conflict in Cuba.

When we learned that the new socialist state had
appeared not far from American shores, I understood
that it would not last long if we didn't help it, so that it
would have time to recover its strength and rest from
the struggle which it had just gone through. And so I
decided, after consulting my colleagues, to send some
rocket units to Cuba. Naturally, before doing this, I put
the question to the members of the Presidium. I told
them: "If we don't do this, Cuba will fall." Many
thought hard about it, and the first to take the floor
was Kosygin, thoughtful and an old Marxist and a real
Leninist. He said, "This is probably a bit adventurous,
but I support you. I can't see any other means of sup-
porting Cuba." After him other members of the Presidium took the floor and backed up my suggestion. We
were sure the Americans would never leave Cuba
alone and let it develop as a socialist country, because
Cuba would act as a magnet to the South American
countries. Sometime in October 1962 the president of
the United States took the floor and said that they had
better take measures.

They concentrated their navy and almost surrounded the island. Then planes were gotten ready
and paratroops and infantry. So they mobilized their

huge forces, and things began to hum. I must confess that I slept one night in my study fully dressed on the sofa. I did not want to be in the position of one Western minister who during the Suez crisis rushed to the telephone without his trousers. The following day, when the conflict was over, I slept quietly in my bed at home.

The American press made a lot of fuss about the Russians bringing rockets to Cuba and planning to capture the United States. Perhaps we shouldn't have done it. But if rockets had not been installed, would there be a Cuba now? No! It would have been wiped out. And if that is true, it means that our transportation of rockets was justified. It cost us money, but we did not lose a single man. We took our rockets and bombers away in exchange for President Kennedy's promise not to invade Cuba. And this should have gained at least six years' quiet, because I was sure Kennedy would have been elected for a second term.

And I am not ashamed that, as the newspapers wrote, I made concessions to the American president in order to remove the rockets from Cuba. We told Comrade Castro and the other comrades that if Kennedy broke his word, all the means that we had are still in our possession and that the threat which he, Castro, held against the United States in defense of Cuba remained in our territory, so that, if the situation required, we could use it.

We must give credit to the United States and, first of all, to President Kennedy, who also showed sense and coolheadedness. He did what he promised—to carry out his part—and we carried out ours. And that's the way we liquidated the possibility of beginning a nuclear war. It is difficult to say what might have happened if we had not shipped the rockets back. Some people say probably there would not have been a war. Probably not. I don't know. I could not give any assurance about that. So who was right and who was wrong? And what was the American aim? The aim to liquidate socialist Cuba. The invasion by the Cuban immigrants was part of the American plan, and our aim was to preserve Cuba, and Cuba still exists. Our action of transporting rockets with nuclear warheads was justified; we brought the breath of war closer to the American warmongers. We also demonstrated a clear understanding of when one can avoid war and solve the question by negotiation. My prestige increased, and this will never fade, and for a long time people will remember it. And even now, when I receive letters at New Year's and Christmas, people usually understand this part.

Cuban refugees squeeze onto a boat during the 1980 Mariel boat lift. Thousands of Cubans fled their homeland to the shores of the United States.

THE CUBAN BOAT LIFT
BY ALEX LARZELERE[38]

On April 1, 1980, a group of Cubans in a bus stormed through the gates of the Peruvian embassy in Havana seeking asylum. One guard was killed.

On April 4, the Cuban government announced that it would no longer risk the lives of its policemen to prevent people from entering the embassy. The guards were withdrawn. Within a few hours the embassy was overcrowded. By April 6 almost ten thousand people were inside its doors.

The situation was an international embarrassment for Fidel Castro, and he offered to let the defectors leave.

U.S. President Jimmy Carter agreed to admit 3,500 people from Cuba and stated that U.S. assistance would be part of an international effort.

On April 20, Havana radio broadcast that the Cuban port of Mariel could be used to receive the coast boats and others sent from Florida to pick up the Cubans who were allowed to leave. By September 125,000 refugees had left for Key West and Miami, Florida.

President Jimmy Carter
Remarks to Reporters
April 9, 1980, Washington, D.C. Our heart goes out to the almost ten thousand freedom-loving Cubans who entered a temporarily open gate at the Peruvian embassy just within this week.

May 14 Tens of thousands are fleeing the repression of the Castro regime under chaotic and perilous conditions. Castro himself has refused to permit them a safe and orderly passage to the United States and to other countries who are willing to receive them. . . . In keeping with the laws and traditions of our country, we offer a safe haven for many of these people who have arrived on our shore. . . . But now we must take additional steps to end Cuba's inhumane actions and bring to safety and order the process that continues to threaten lives.

Wayne S. Smith
U.S. diplomat in Cuba, April 6 They sat on the roof and trees and crammed every square foot of the compound [roughly the size of a city block]. Other thousands converged from all over the island. Trains and buses disgorged passengers, usually with cardboard suitcases in hand, who headed straight for the Peruvian embassy.

When on April 7, the compound was filled to capacity, a police cordon was thrown around it to keep new arrivals out. Fights erupted between police and those still trying to get in. From inside, those who had already made it jeered the police and shouted encouragement to those trying to break through. Castro again came to have a look and, according to a newsman who was there at the time, was shaken by what he saw. He may at that point have realized that he had miscalculated. A great tear had suddenly appeared in his orderly, regimented socialist society.

Editorial in *Granma* (a Havana newspaper)
May 19, 1980 Criminals have left here, and we have said so repeatedly. We have publicly made it clear that a great majority of those who went into the Peruvian

embassy were not "dissidents" but criminals. There are cries now that the United States does not want to become a garbage dump for Cuban scum. . . . The United States is solely responsible for having encouraged these elements to leave Cuba and to go to that country. This is why so many of them feel they are entitled to U.S. hospitality. It would not be fair to let them down.

Jimmy Carter, Washington, D.C.   In the spring and summer I had to deal with a stream of illegal Cuban refugees who began coming to our country. We welcomed the first ones to freedom, but when the stream became a torrent, I explored every legal means to control the badly deteriorating situation. Even so, it was impossible to stop them all. . . . I sympathized with the plight of the refugees, but they were coming in illegally, and I was sworn to uphold the law of our land.

Cuban army colonel
Mariel, September 25, 1980   Good morning. Mariel is closed. You must go.

Fidel Castro, Havana, Cuba
December 1980   Mariel has not been resolved; it has simply been suspended.

Three or four thousand of these people were criminals or mentally ill individuals. A year or so later, they were returned in exchange for long-term exiled Cuban prisoners.

The majority of the Mariel boat-lift people in Florida are still waiting impatiently for the collapse of the Fidel Castro regime in the hope of being able to return to their homeland.

A NAZI PRISON
IN THE CARIBBEAN
BY ARMANDO VALLADERES[39]

Armando Valladeres, a young Cuban poet, was arrested in 1963 by Castro's secret police. His only crime: he was philosophically opposed to communism. After twenty-two years of savage imprisonment, he was released through the personal intervention of President François Mitterrand of France.

The excerpt that follows is taken from Valladeres's book, *Against All Hope*. In it he describes a typical prison day with its beatings, its anguish, and its courage to endure. Today Armando Valladeres is living in exile in Spain.

At sunrise the garrison flooded the hallway. They came in shouting. It was the same always; they had to get all heated up to come in. They beat on the walls and on the bars with the weapons they were carrying— rubber-hose-covered iron bars (so they would not break the skin), thick clubs, and woven elastic cables, chains wrapped around their hands, and bayonets. There was no justification, no pretext. They just opened cells, one by one, and beat the prisoners inside. The first cell they opened was Martin Perez. I remember his big husky voice, cursing the Communists, but without saying a single dirty word. I got close to the bars to try to look out, and a chain blow made me jump back. I was lucky it had not hit me in the face.

They opened cell number 3, number 4, number 5. As they then approached my cell, I trembled inside. My muscles contracted spasmodically. My breathing came with difficulty and I felt the fear and rage that always possessed me. Some men, their psychological resistance wasted away already, could not contain themselves, and before the soldiers even entered their cells, they began to shriek and wail hysterically. Those shrieks multiplied the horror. The soldiers even entered their cells armed with bayonets; behind the main guard were three more, blocking the entrance.

I saw only that one of the guards was carrying a chain. They pushed us to the back of the cell so they would have room to swing their weapons. We tried not to get separated because we knew that was the most dangerous thing you could do. That was the reason they would find to kick you and maybe knee you in the groin. They knocked me to the floor, and one of them kicked me in the face and split my lower lip. Even when I recovered consciousness my head was lying in a pool of blood. My cell mate was bleeding through the nose, and his hand was fractured at the wrist.

Several men were seriously injured. One of the Graino brothers had his cheekbone fractured by Sergeant "Good Guy"; he spit out broken teeth. He had been beaten so brutally that his face looked like one huge ball of black eye. Fechuguita, a peaceable little campesino from Pinar del Rio, had his head split open; the wound was so large it took twenty stitches to close it. Every man without exception was beaten. The guards went about it systematically, cell by cell.

After the beating the officers and a military doctor passed through to examine us. They took wounded men out of the cells, but right there on the spot a medic with a little first-aid cart sewed up and bandaged the wounds. When they finished bandaging us, they said, "Don't say we didn't give you medical treatment," and put us back into the cells, where we waited for our next beating.

I was bruised all over. My face was swollen and bloody. I could hardly stand up for the pain all over my body. They had given me the worst beating of my life. But what had affected me most was waiting for them to come to my cell and beat me. That did more damage to me than the blows themselves. A thousand times I wished I had been in the first cell. That way they would come in, beat me, and go back out again. I wanted it over with once and for all so I wouldn't have to go through that torture of waiting and dreading. My nerves were destroyed by it.

The guards came back in the afternoon, almost at nightfall, and the nightmare of the morning was repeated, beatings, cell by cell, with more wounded men the results. We could at least communicate with the other sections of the building by shouting back and forth, so we traded the names of the most gravely wounded men. Odilo Alonso woke up the next morning with his head monstrously swollen. I would never have imagined that anyone could look so grotesquely deformed. His ears were so swollen he looked as though he were wearing a helmet. After three days of those two-a-day beatings, many men could no longer stand. Martin Perez was urinating blood, as was De Vera, and other men's eyes were so blackened and swollen shut by the blows that they could hardly see. But that didn't matter to the soldiers—they beat men again and again.

Sergeant Good Guy, whose real name was Ismael, belonged to the Communist party. He had a big Panco mustache. Whenever the garrison came to beat us, he cried, *"Viva comunismo!"* madly over and over. It was his war cry. He would tell the other soldiers to beat the wounded on top of their bandages, so that nobody could say that the soldiers had beaten them more than once. Another sergeant did exactly the opposite—he would beat the wounded men on their bare skin and say with a sneer, "I wanna see 'em sew you up again."

Odilo was getting worse and worse. The blows to

MIAMI, 1986
BY JOAN DIDION[40]

Only ninety miles distant from the island of Cuba, Miami has a long history of involvement in Cuban-American affairs. From 1895, when the exiled José Martí (after whom Radio Martí is named) raised money from Cuban tobacco workers to fund his revolutionary plans, until 1955 when Fidel Castro arrived in Miami to solicit support for his revolution, this American city has had a long history of harboring patriots in exile and sheltering Cubans of every kind.

Nobody writes with more authority of this Cuban-American city than Joan Didion. After many trips to Miami and countless talks and interviews with both American and Cuban residents in all walks of life, she has given us a masterly picture of Miami's turbulent and cosmopolitan citizenry.

The excerpt that follows provides an insight into the multicultural life of this American city which is, in its way, also an outpost of Cuba.

In fact, 43 percent of the population of Dade County was by that time [1986] "Hispanic," which meant mostly Cuban. Fifty-six percent of the population of Miami itself was Hispanic. The most visible new buildings on the Miami skyline, the Arquitectonico buildings along Brickell Avenue, were built by a firm with a Cuban founder. There were Cubans in the boardrooms of the major banks, Cubans in the clubs that did not admit Jews or blacks, and four Cubans in the most recent mayoralty campaigns. Suarez had beaten out the incumbent and all other candidates to meet in a run-off.

A real-life bystander merges with the painted images of a mural in Miami's Little Havana section. Located only 90 miles from Cuba, Miami has had a long history of involvement in Cuban-American affairs.

The entire tone of the city, the way the people looked and talked and met one another, was Cuban. The very image the city had begun presenting of itself, what was then its newfound glamour, its "hotness" (hot colors, hot vice, shady dealings under palm trees), was that of prerevolutionary Havana as perceived by Americans. There was even in the way women dressed in Miami a definable Havana look, a more distinct emphasis on the hips and décolletage, more black, more veiling, a generalized flirtatiousness of style not then current in American cities. I recall being struck, during an afternoon spent at La Liga contra Cáncer, a prominent exile charity which raises money to help cancer patients, by the appearance of the volunteers who had met that day to stuff envelopes for a benefit. Their hair was sleek, of slightly other period, immaculate pageboys and French twists. They wore Bruno Magli pumps and silk and linen dresses of considerable expense. There seemed to be a preference for strictest gray or black, but the effect remained lush, tropical, like a roomful of perfectly groomed mangoes.

This was not, in other words, an invisible 56 percent of the population. Even the social notes in *Diario Las Americas* and in *El Herald*, the daily Spanish edition of the *Herald*, written and edited for *el exilio*, suggested a dominant culture, one with money to spend, a notable willingness to spend it in public. Almost any day it was possible to drive past the limestone arches and fountains which marked the boundaries of Coral Gables and see little girls being photographed in the tiaras and ruffled hoop skirts and maribou-trimmed illusion capes they would wear at their *quinces*, the elaborate fifteenth birthday parties at which the community's female children came of official age. The favored backdrop was one suggesting Castilian grandeur, which was how the Coral Gables arches happened to figure. Since the idealization of the virgin implicit in the *quince* could only exist in the presence of its natural foil, machismo, there was often a brother around, or a boyfriend. There was also a mother, in dark glasses, not only to protect the symbolic virgin but to point out the better angle, the more aristocratic location. The quinceanera would pick up her hoop skirts and move as directed, often revealing the scuffed jellies she had worn that day to school. A few weeks later she would be transformed in *Diario Las Americas*, one of the morning battalion of smoldering fifteen-year-olds, each with her arch, her fountain, her borrowed scenery, the gift if not exactly the intention of the late George Merrick who built the arches when he developed Coral Gables. . . .

Cubans were perceived as most satisfactory when they appeared to most fully share the aspirations and manners of middle-class Americans, at the same time adding "color" to the city on appropriate occasions—for example, at their *quinces* (the *quinces* were one aspect of Cuban life almost invariably mentioned by Anglos who tended to present them as evidence of Cuban irresponsibility, or childishness), or on the day of the annual Calle Ocho Festival, when they could, according to the *Herald*, "samba" in the streets and stir up a paella for two thousand (10 cooks, 2,000 mussels, 220 pounds of lobster, and 440 pounds of rice), using rowboat oars as spoons. Cubans were perceived as least satisfactory when they "acted clannish," "kept to themselves," "had their own ways," and, two frequent flash points, "spoke Spanish when they didn't need to" and frequently got "political," complaints, each of them, which suggested an Anglo view of what Cubans should be, at significant odds with what Cubans were.

HAVANA: AUGUST 1991
JOSE DE CORDOBA[41]

José de Cordoba, reporting to his paper, the *Wall Street Journal*, quotes Manuel Davis, a senior foreign ministry official, as saying, "There is an obsession about food [in Cuba], there is a tension about food. But everybody in Cuba gets a piece of bread daily."

Housing shortages continue to plague Cubans. Here, a couple is shown in their small two-room apartment in Havana.

In his article, de Cordoba enlarges on that theme. Hungry people wait in long lines, he reports, while others wait in line for hours at the U.S. consulate hoping to obtain visitors' visas which the United States no longer gives.

Haunted by hunger, fearful of the future, the Cuban people are still dominated by Fidel Castro while fearing his secret forces, which are thought to be omnipresent. The picture of Cuba as of August 27, 1991, is grim. There is small hope that the situation will improve.

In shabby San Lazaro Street, a few blocks from the magnificent steps of the University of Havana, the day of "zero option" looks closer. No one has seen meat here for two months. So when word spreads before dawn . . . that meat and fish are to be had, a line of people, mostly elderly women clutching worn cloth shopping bags, forms in front of a dimly lighted empty bodega.

At nine o'clock, an elderly man in a porkpie hat and *guaya bera* [T-shirt] shuffles out of the shop gripping a small paper bag full of little fish. "I've been waiting since four in the morning," says Marlo, a retired construction worker, who, like most people here, is reluctant to offer up his surname for publication. A woman looking on as he pulls a fish from the bag comments: "After you cut off the head and clean it, it won't get you very far. Soon we will be eating dirt."

A block away, another line stretches around the corner. There people wait somberly for their ration of daily bread—one tough little yellow roll made from scarce imported Soviet wheat. Down the street is the long line for eggplant, the vegetable of the day, and still another line for milk.

Most times, Cuba is like *Waiting for Godot*, but with a cast of ten million spending their lives waiting. Rations have dwindled to five pounds of rice a month, five eggs a week, and a quarter chicken per person every nine days. When the ration is used up or supplies run short, as often happens, people wait for up to two hours to get the carbohydrates supplied by the cheap, dreadful pizzas. A lot of people also are in line to emigrate to the United States, but it has stopped processing visitors, most likely to increase pressure on Mr. Castro.

Haunted by the fear of hunger, Cuban society continues to be dominated by Mr. Castro—and paralyzed by fear of his security forces, which are thought to be everywhere. The regime has been able to internalize repression. On every block, a Committee for the Defense of the Revolution takes notes on the comings and goings of visitors. Except for a few dissidents who feel they have little to lose, this remains a country of anonymous people, afraid to speak their minds in public.

After thirty-two years in power, Mr. Castro remains a towering figure here, however out of touch he may be with the young and with the swirl of change throughout the former Communist world. Almost 60 percent of the Cuban population was born after he came to power in 1959. "He's crazy," says a thirty-year-old playwright, holding a finger to his head.

"He's senile," says a Soviet-educated engineer called Melba. But in the next breath Melba says she would "tremble if Mr. Castro were to enter the room."

"I still admire him," says a twenty-year-old colleague of hers. And despite the hardships, many older Cubans particularly retain a profound sense of loyalty to the unbending leader.

A poster of Havana Libre Hotel is a collage of photographs of Cuban sights—including a mountain, a mass rally, and the sea. The legend at the bottom reads like a drumroll of the regime's worst fears: "This won't fall. This won't tremble. This won't fade."

Recently the government urged Cubans, with mixed results to join ominously named "rapid-action detachments"—revolutionary vigilantes who are supposed to convince malcontents of the error of their ways. "They explained it wasn't a civil war or anything like that," says Alejandro, a young mechanic whose mother signed him up. He says that as a battalion member he is supposed to defend the revolution if anyone criticizes it in public. Would he use violence? "I'd plan to get lost," he says.

A bread riot might detonate violence. Screaming

In 1992, two young girls play as adults wait in line for supplies. Aid to Cuba from the former Soviet Union had ceased because of the political changes in that country.

arguments are a constant in the food lines. Many families in Havana say they are eating just once a day. While schools and many employers serve lunch, some factories and offices are letting people go early, so as not to have to serve a meal. A recipe making the rounds in Havana is for a steak substitute of boiled and breaded grapefruit rind. "We are not starving, but we are not living either," says a young theater director.

FIDEL CASTRO, PRESIDENT OF CUBA, VISITS THE U.N.

On October 25, 1995, the State Department granted Fidel Castro a five day visa to New York to attend the Fiftieth Anniversary of the United Nations General Assembly celebration, his first visit in 16 years.

Clad in a dark business suit, forced on him by the diplomatic community, he made a six-minute speech in which he attacked new colonialism. An excerpt from his speech follows.

The Cold War is over. But the arms race goes on. And nuclear and military hegemonism perpetuate themselves. How long shall we wait for the total removal of all weapons of mass extermination, for universal disarmament, and for the elimination of the use of force, arrogance, and pressure in international relations?

The obsolete veto privilege and the ill use of the Security Council by the powerful are exalting a new colonialism within the very United Nations. Latin America and Africa do not have one single permanent member on the Security Council. In Asia, India has a population of almost one billion, but it does not enjoy that responsibility.

We lay claim to a world without hegemonism, without nuclear weapons, without intervention, without racism, without national or religious hatred, without

Fidel Castro waves to the crowd during a visit to France in 1995. There continues to be much speculation about Cuba's future once Castro steps down as president of Cuba.

outrageous acts against the sovereignty of any country—a world of respect for the independence and self-determination of peoples—a world without universal models that totally disregard the traditions and culture of all the components of mankind.

We lay claim to a world without ruthless blockades that cause the death of men, women, and children, youths and elders, like noiseless atom bombs. We lay claim to a world of peace, justice, and dignity where everyone without exception has the right to well-being and to life.

Outside the U.N. hundreds of Cuban-Americans chanted for his death. One person carried a poster of Hitler, Stalin, and Castro. Flotillas of pro- and anti-Castro demonstrators moved at cross currents in the East River.

Castro gave a one and a half hour interview to the editors and reporters of *The Wall Street Journal*. Castro praised the U.S. business community as more efficient and reliable than the diplomats and politicians, some of whom snubbed him during his New York visit. Mayor Giuliani and President Clinton excluded Castro from their official receptions.

Mr. Castro said, "it seems to be better to develop relations with big businessmen because they are enormously powerful. . . . A lifting of the 33-year-old embargo would be a major challenge for him and his government. If our country is flooded with American tourists and businessmen, it's likely we would be sent to the mad house because we would not be able to handle it." But, he then acknowledged there would be little chance of that because embargo tightening legislation has turned relations between the two countries into a "Gordian knot."

After a restrained day of diplomacy, Castro changed back into fatigues and spent the evening before an enthusiastic audience at the Abyssinian Baptist Church in Harlem.

"This is the 35th anniversary of my first visit to this neighborhood, and the incredible thing is, I am still expelled. I am still being left out of the dinners as if nothing had changed in all these years, as if we were still in the days of the cold war."
In Miami, watching Mr. Castro's appearance at the United Nations on television, many Cuban exiles said they were chilled by the warm reception he received.

The aging bad boy Fidel Castro got most of the pre-celebration air time, no doubt largely because he was not accorded a friendly welcome by the U.N.

CUBA SHOOTS DOWN AMERICAN PLANES

January 29, 1996
Cuban air force jets shot down two civilian planes off the northeast coast of Cuba. A third plane escaped and returned to Miami. The U.S. planes belonged to a Cuban exile group based in Miami, called Brothers to the Rescue. Four American pilots were killed.

President Clinton outraged, ordered the American interest section in Havana to give an explanation.

The aircraft that were downed were unarmed. The Miami-based Cuban aircraft group specializes in rescuing, from the straits of Florida, refugees who seek to flee Cuba by craft to reach the United States.

The United States called an emergency meeting at the U.N. Warren Christopher, the U.S. secretary of state, said, "The Cuban fighter jets failed to warn the U.S. pilots which were in violation of international law."

Mrs. Albright, the U.S. representative, said, "I was struck by the joy of the Cuban pilots committing cold-blooded murder and bragging of their success. Frankly it is not a success, it is cowardice."

Congressional negotiators and President Clinton agreed on a package of sanctions intended to punish President Castro by curbing foreign investments in Cuba. Other measures were also under consideration. Supporters of these measures in the U.S. believe that they may hasten the downfall of the ailing Castro regime.

President Clinton commenting on the affair: "Saturday's attack was an appalling reminder of the nature of the Cuban regime; repressive, violent, and scornful of international law."

February 2–7
José de Cordoba staff reporter of the *Wall Street Journal* wrote: "A senior official said they were searching for steps that would punish Castro, but not the Cuban people or their relatives in the U.S. But it is not easy."

The incident followed a week in which Cuban police arrested 100 dissidents and human rights activists who were seeking a peaceful dialogue with the Castro government.

A Cuban general said that the decision to shoot down the two unarmed planes could have been made only by President Castro.

The shooting down of the planes together with the crackdown on the dissidents is also a clear sign to Cubans that the regime will deal with any other dissidents ruthlessly.

Foreign investment is still prohibited in the areas of defense, national security, education, and public health, although a foreign investment will be allowed in businesses run by the armed forces. And foreign investments still require case by case approval by Cuban Council Administrators.

The crucial sugar harvest, heavily mortgaged to foreign banks, is unlikely to hit the government's 4.5 million-ton goal. A new confrontation with the U.S. will give Castro yet another excuse to explain why the harvest has again failed.

The only way the embargo can ever be lifted is if Castro leaves Cuba.

Source Notes

1 New York Press Society, 1892.
2. Charles E. Chapman, *A History of the Cuban Republic* (Los Angeles: Octagon, 1969).
3. *New York Herald*, November 5, 1873.
4. Gonzalo de Quesada, *The War in Cuba* (Liberty, 1898).
5. José Martí article in *Patria*, official organ of the Cuban Revolutionary Party in the United States, 1895.
6. José Martí, "A Vindication of Cuba," *New York Evening Post*, March 25, 1889.
7. Winston Churchill, *A Roving Commission* (New York: Scribners, 1930).
8. José Martí, *Autobiography of José Martí* (Havana, 1943).
9. Gonzalo de Quesada, *The War in Cuba* (Liberty, 1898).
10. Grover Flint, *Marching with Gomez* (Lamson, Wolf & Co., 1898).
11. Ibid.
12. Gonzalo de Quesada, *The War in Cuba* (Liberty, 1898).
13. Richard Harding Davis, *The Fate of the Pacificos* (R. H. Russel & Co., 1897).
14. Johnny O'Brien, *A Captain Unafraid* (New York: Harper and Brothers, 1897).
15. Gonzalo de Quesada, *Cuba's Great Struggle for Freedom* (Liberty, 1898).
16. *New York Herald*, February 15, 1898.
17. Official document, March 28, 1898.
18. Richard Harding Davis, *The Charge of San Juan Hill* (R. H. Russel & Co. 1897).

19. Leonard Wood, *How Cuba Won Self-Determination* (New York: Doubleday, 1920).

20. Major William C. Gorgas, *Report of the Department of Sanitation: Yellow Fever* (Riggs Publishing Co., 1902).

21. Sumner Welles, *The Time for Decision* (New York: Harper and Brothers, 1944).

22. Speech by Fidel Castro, October 16, 1953.

23. José Llovio Menedez, *My Hidden Life as a Revolutionary* (New York: Bantam, 1938).

24. Warren Hinckle and William Turner, *The Fish is Red* (New York: HarperCollins, 1981).

25. Tad Szulc, *Fidel: A Critical Portrait* (New York: Morrow, 1986).

26. H. L. Matthews, *The Cuban Story* (New York: George Braziller, 1961).

27. Fulgencio Batista, *Cuba Betrayed* (New York: Vantage, 1962).

28. Nicholas Rivero, *Castro's Cuba: An American Dilemma* (Bridgeport, CT.: Luce).

29. G. A. Gey, *Guerrilla Prince* (Boston: Little Brown, 1991).

30. Howard Hunt, *Give Us This Day* (New York: Crown, 1973).

31. Howard Hunt, *The Bay of Pigs* (New York: Crown, 1973).

32. James Monahan and Kenneth Gilmore, *The Great Deception* (New York: Farrar Straus & Giroux, 1963).

33. James Monahan and Kenneth Gilmore, *The Cárdenas Affair* (New York: Farrar Straus & Giroux, 1963).

34. Speech, October 22, 1962.

35. Pedro Manuel Barera with Roberto Fuentes, "The Sugar Harvest," *Cuba* magazine, Havana, 1965.

36. Ernesto "Che" Guevara, *Selected Speeches and Writings* (New York: Merit, 1967).

37. Radio address, July 11, 1967.

38. Alex Larzelere, *The 1980 Cuban Boat Lift* (Washington, D.C.: National Defense University Press, 1988).

39. Armando Valladeres, *Against All Hope* (New York: Knopf, 1986).

40. Joan Didion, *Miami* (New York: Simon & Schuster, 1987).

41. José de Cordoba, "Havana: August 1991," *The Wall Street Journal,* August 27, 1991.

CHRONOLOGY

1492   Christopher Columbus anchors his ships off the coast of Cuba; Columbus claims Cuba as a Spanish possession despite its estimated 200,000 Ciboney and Arawak inhabitants

1511   Diego Velázquez establishes the first permanent Spanish settlement at Baracoa

1519   Havana, founded four years earlier, moves to its current site

1550s   Gold is discovered in Cuba

1620   The *Mayflower* lands at Plymouth Rock on December 11

1776   The United States claims independence from England on July 4

1814   Ferdinand VII is restore to the Spanish throne

1853   Poet and patriot José Martí is born in Havana on January 28

1861   The U.S. Civil War begins

1868   Carlos Manuel de Céspedes leads a major revolt known as the Ten Years' War

1873   The *Virginius* is seized by Spanish authorities; all 53 crew members, including some Americans, are executed

1876   Spain sends General Arsenio Martínez to crush the revolution

1878   The Pact of Zanjón ends the Ten Years' War

1886   Spain grants Cuba representation in the Spanish parliament and abolishes slavery in Cuba

1889   Martí's "A Vindication of Cuba" is published in the New York *Evening Post*

1894   Spain cancels a trade pact between Cuba and the United States; the United States' retaliatory tariff on Cuban sugar severely depresses the Cuban economy

1895 A second war of independence erupts in Cuba; Martí dies on May 19

1986 Spain sends General Valeriano Weyler ("The Butcher") to quell the rebellion; Weyler institutes his *reconcentrado* policy

1898 The U.S. battleship *Maine* explodes and sinks in Havana harbor on February 15; U.S. Congress votes to declare war on Spain on April 25; Spain surrenders in August; a peace treaty is signed in December

1899 The United States begins its occupation of Cuba; U.S. general Leonard Wood is appointed military governor of Cuba

1900 A yellow fever epidemic sweeps through Cuba

1901 The first Cuban constitution is drafted; Cubans are forced to accept the Platt Amendment, which allows the United States to build a naval base at Guantánamo Bay

1902 U.S. military rule over Cuba ends (U.S. Navy maintains its Guantánamo Bay base); Tómas Estrada Palma is elected as the first president of Cuba

1924 Gerardo Machado is elected as president of Cuba

1926 Fidel Castro is born on August 13 near Birán, Cuba

1930 The world sugar market collapses

1933 U.S. president Franklin Roosevelt appoints Sumner Welles as ambassador to Cuba; Machado is overthrown

1940 Fulgencio Batista is elected president

1944 Ramón Grau is elected president

1952 Batista orchestrates a military coup and seizes control of the Cuban government

1953 Fidel Castro and 125 student rebels attempt a coup against the Batista regime on July 26;

Castro is arrested and sentenced to 15 years in prison

1955   Batista grants a general amnesty to the student revolutionaries, freeing Castro

1956   Castro returns to Cuba aboard the *Granma* on December 2

1957   A group of students led by José Echeverría attacks the presidential palace on March 13 in an attempt to kill Batista

1958   Batista meets with military leaders on December 31 to announce his resignation

1959   Castro and his revolutionaries march triumphantly into Havana on January 8; Castro meets with U.S. vice president Richard Nixon in April

1961   The unsuccessful Bay of Pigs invasion occurs in April

1962   Anticommunist demonstrators are overwhelmed in Cárdenas; U.S. president John Kennedy delivers a television address on October 22 about the Soviet missile bases being built in Cuba

1966   Che Guevara is killed in Bolivia

1975   Cuba sends troops to Angola to assist Soviet-supported forces

1980   Nearly 125,000 Cuban refugees arrive in the United States during the Mariel boat lift

1985   U.S. broadcasts to Cuba on Radio Martí begin

1991   Soviet aid to Cuba is reduced

1995   Fidel Castro attends the fiftieth-anniversary celebrations at the United Nations in New York City

1996   Cuban air force jets shoot down two civilian planes owned by the Miami-based Brothers to the Rescue on January 28

For Further Reading

Appel, Ted. *José Martí*. New York: Chelsea House, 1992.

Batista, Fulgencio. *Growth and Decline of the Cuban Republic*. Greenwich, CT: Devin-Adair, 1964.

Beyer, Don. *Castro!* New York: Franklin Watts, 1993.

Blight, James G., et al. *Cuba on the Brink: Castro, the Missile Crisis, and the Soviet Collapse*. New York: St. Martins, 1994.

Blow, Michael. *Ship to Remember: The Maine and the Spanish-American War*. New York: Morrow, 1992.

Castro, Fidel. *History Will Absolve Me*. New York: Carol, 1961.

Chapman, Charles E. *A History of the Cuban Republic*. Los Angeles: Octagon Books, 1969.

Cuba: A Country Study, 3d edition. Washington, D.C.: U.S. Government Printing Office, 1988.

Didion, Joan. *Miami*. New York: Simon & Schuster, 1987.

Geldof, Lynn. *The Cubans: Voices of Change*. New York: St. Martins, 1992.

Gernand, Renee. *Cuban Americans*. New York: Chelsea House, 1989.

Geyer, Georgie Anne. *Guerrilla Prince*. Boston: Little, Brown, 1991.

Higgins, Turnbull. *The Perfect Failure: Kennedy, Eisenhower, and the CIA at the Bay of Pigs*. New York: Norton, 1989.

Hinckle, Warren and William Turner. *The Fish is Red*. New York: HarperCollins, 1981.

Kennedy, Robert F. *Thirteen Days: A Memoir of the Cuban Missile Crisis*. New York: NAL-Dutton, 1969.

Martí, José. *Discursos Selectos de José Martí.* Miami: Ediciones Universal, 1977. [Spanish-language]

Medina, Pablo. *Exiled Memories: A Cuban Childhood.* Austin: University of Texas Press, 1990.

Mendez, Adriana. *Cubans in America.* Minneapolis: Lerner, 1994.

Michener, James A. and John Kings. *Six Days in Havana.* Austin: University of Texas Press, 1989.

Offner, John L. *An Unwanted War: The Diplomacy of the United States and Spain over Cuba, 1895–1898.* Chapel Hill: University of North Carolina Press, 1992.

Pando, Magdalen M. *Cuba's Freedom Fighter, Antonio Maceo.* Melrose, FL: Felicity, 1980.

Rice, Earle, Jr. *Cuban Revolution.* San Diego: Lucent, 1994.

Rieff, David. *The Exile: Cuba in the Heart of Miami.* New York: Simon and Schuster, 1993.

Szulc, Tad. *Fidel: A Critical Protrait.* New York: Morrow, 1986.

Valladeres, Armando. *Against All Hope.* New York: Knopf, 1986.

Williams, Stephen. *Cuba: The Land, the History, the People, the Culture.* Philadelphia: Running Press, 1994.

Index

About the Authors

Rhoda Hoff was educated at the Brearley School and Barnard College. Married to the explorer Helmut de Terra, she accompanied him on three expeditions to Ladakh, Java, and Burma on behalf of Yale University. Later, she traveled to Africa with Father Pierre Teilhard de Chardin for the Wenner-Gren Foundation to report about the work being done on early humans. Rhoda Hoff has written 16 books for young people as well as two novels. She lives in Washington, D.C.

Margaret Regler attended the Farmington School and was cofounder of the progressive school, *Miquon*, which is still flourishing. She was married to the German writer Gustav Regler and lived in Europe until his death. Margaret Regler now divides her time between New York and Mexico, where she assists the distinguished archaeologist, Alezander von Wuthenau.